THE
CUSTOMER
DIFFERENTIAL

THE
CUSTOMER
DIFFERENTIAL

The Complete Guide
to Implementing
Customer Relationship
Management

Melinda Nykamp

AMACOM
American Management Association
New York • Atlanta • Boston • Chicago • Kansas City • San Francisco • Washington, D.C.
Brussels • Mexico City • Tokyo • Toronto

Special discounts on bulk quantities of AMACOM books are available to corporations, professional associations, and other organizations. For details, contact Special Sales Department, AMACOM, a division of American Management Association, 1601 Broadway, New York, NY 10019.
Tel.: 212-903-8316. Fax: 212-903-8083.
Web Site: www. amacombooks.org

This publication is designed to provide accurate and authoritative information in regard to the subject matter covered. It is sold with the understanding that the publisher is not engaged in rendering legal, accounting, or other professional service. If legal advice or other expert assistance is required, the services of a competent professional person should be sought.

Library of Congress Cataloging-in-Publication Data

Nykamp, Melinda.
    The customer differential : the complete guide to implementing customer relationship management / Melinda Nykamp.
        p. cm.
    Includes index.
    ISBN 0-8144-0622-X
    1. Customer relations—Management. 2. Data mining. 1. Title.

HF5415.5 .N947 2001
658.8'12—dc21

                                                            00–050226

Printing number

10 9 8 7 6 5 4 3 2 1

CONTENTS

THE
CUSTOMER
DIFFERENTIAL

CHAPTER ONE

CRM:
WHAT IT'S REALLY ALL ABOUT

Imagine a world in which you could readily locate and purchase the products and services that you need, coupled with receiving ongoing relevant communications and amazing service and support. Imagine that the provider understood:

- The products that are most relevant to you
- The price you are willing to pay
- The most effective way of communicating with you
- The level of service and support that you expect, and your preferred channels
- Their value to you, and your value to them
- What it would take to increase your loyalty

What if the provider not only knew this information, but also was willing and able to readily, consistently, and effectively act on this information? You would have an optimal shopping and service experience—every day! This is the promise of customer relationship management (CRM). For customers, the result is increased relevance and value. For service providers, the result is what I am terming the *customer differential*; essentially a new level of competitive differentiation through impermeable customer relationships.

Since many of you are likely frequent flyers, let's consider your ongoing relationship with airlines and assess how they manage their relationship with you, the customer. Let's assume that the leading provider in your area is Acme Airlines. If you fly frequently, your relationship with Acme most likely vacillates between exceptional and downright devastating.

On a positive note:

- They typically get you where you need to go safely and on time.
- They offer you a wide range of vacation-package specials, some of which are of interest to you.
- They have the Acme Frequent Flyer Program, which provides you with ongoing recognition, convenience, and special privileges for your loyalty. Some of these rewards include a frequent flyer card and T-shirt, designated check-in desks at the airport, the opportunity to board the plane early, a special toll-free number that promises a shorter wait time, and occasional upgrades. Acme also issues points that can be redeemed for free travel.
- Acme also has a variety of partners that provide you with some of the same recognition, conveniences, and special privileges, as well as rewards.

On the flip side:

- The process of tracking, claiming, and redeeming Acme points for free travel has proved to be a headache. The department in charge of this process doesn't seem to realize who you are or what you mean to Acme Airlines.

- The Acme–cobranded credit card provider also does not seem to care about your relationship with Acme Airlines or your loyalty to them.
- You have been to the Acme website three times now; it does not really seem to provide the customized experience that they advertise.
- Six weeks ago you e-mailed a complaint regarding a ticketing mistake to Acme's online customer service team and still have not received a response.
- Even though you are a very frequent flier on Acme, you do not seem to be rewarded preferential treatment by gate agents for discretionary services such as seat assignments, upgrades, or any other amenities.
- Acme's travel agent partners seem to sometimes be at odds with the airline. Acme leaves you on your own if you booked through an agent and is wary of offering any service or support.

If you were to summarize your overall relationship with Acme Airlines, you would probably say that it is all right; or you might even say that it is a love-hate relationship depending on the situation. Acme seems to have good intentions and is proactive in developing sales and marketing promotions. However, they often fall short in their ongoing delivery of service and support.

What could Acme Airlines do to secure your business and move you from being a lukewarm customer to a consistently satisfied loyal customer? How could your relationship with Acme be improved?

CRM suggests that a consistent, positive customer experience across all channels and media and across all sales, marketing, and service functions can increase customer loyalty and advocacy. CRM is designed to be a win-win: Customers receive the shopping and service experience that they deserve; the provider receives ongoing loyalty resulting in increased business.

We all have our own personal shopping and service "horror stories"—the phone rep who insulted your intelligence . . . the special promotion that was impossible to redeem . . . the loyalty program that only captured a third of your total activity, and then rewarded you with irrelevant marketing promotions. The key question is, how can you as a provider prevent those experiences that you as a customer would never want to encounter? Moreover, how can you as a provider ensure that your customers have nothing short of wonderful shopping and service experiences?

If you are successful with CRM strategies, you can expect to rapidly gain a unique competitive advantage—you will have customers on your side. This customer differential is the key to success in the twenty-first century.

CRM Defined

CRM is suddenly the talk of the town. It is a worldwide focus on customers, covered now in popular media and within corporate boardrooms around the world. Never before has there been such a focus on keeping customers coming back. Perhaps the closest business movement was the customer satisfaction efforts of the 1980s. These customer satisfaction initiatives, however, often ended with common means of measuring, but not necessarily improving, customer satisfaction. CRM is much broader than the age-old principle that "the customer is always right." CRM identifies how to profitably act on that premise, at all times, across all channels and functions.

CRM is essentially a focus on providing optimal value to your customers—through the way you communicate with them, how you market to them, and how you service them—as well as through the traditional means of product, price, promotion, and place of distribution (see Figure 1-1). Customers make buying decisions based on more than just price and more than just product. Customers make buying decisions based on their overall experience, which involves product and price, but also includes the nature of all their interactions with you. If you can consistently deliver on these marketing, sales, service, and support interactions, you will be richly rewarded with ongoing customer loyalty and value; therein lies significant competitive advantage.

Figure 1-1. Shift in focus.

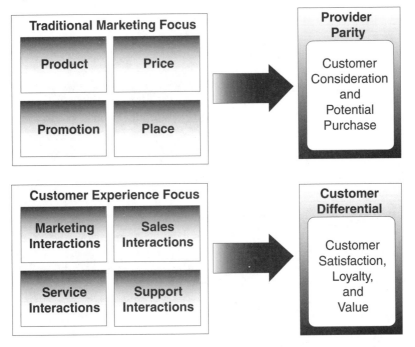

The CRM Process

There is a universal, underlying cycle of activity that should drive all CRM initiatives. All initiatives and infrastructure development should somehow be linked to this core cycle of activity, as shown in Figure 1-2. As a cycle, the stages are interdependent and continuous. They are *interdependent* in that you cannot implement some stages without the others. Consider that:

- Customization of products and services for customers requires an understanding of who your customers are
- Interaction and delivery of increased value to customers requires development and customization of products and services to meet their needs
- Retention of customers requires this delivery of increased value

Figure 1-2. The CRM process.

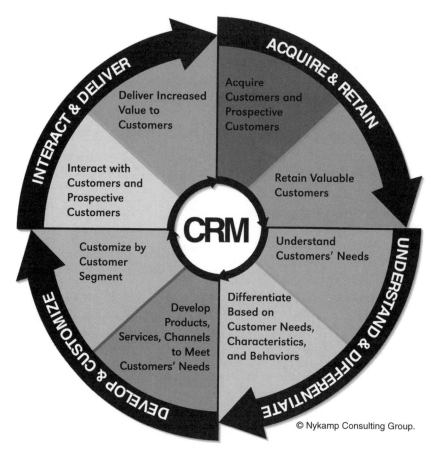

© Nykamp Consulting Group.

The cycle is *continuous* in that relationships by their nature involve an ongoing series of interactions. As you repeat this cycle with any customer or group of customers:

- Your CRM strategies and initiatives will become increasingly sophisticated.
- Customers will take notice of what you are doing for them.
- You will thereby benefit from increased customer satisfaction, loyalty, and profitability, provided that you continue the cycle and continue to invest in customer relationships. As you move from one stage to the next, you

gain insight and understanding that supports and enhances your subsequent efforts.

As shown in the cycle, for any organization, business starts with the acquisition of customers. However, any successful CRM initiative is highly dependent on a solid understanding of customers. Thus, our discussion starts there.

Understand and Differentiate

You cannot have a relationship with customers unless you understand them—what they value, what services are important to them, how and when they prefer to interact, and what they want to buy. Customer understanding involves:

- *Customer Profiling.* This process identifies customer demographic and geographic characteristics such as age, size of household, and proximity to your nearest retail location. If you are profiling businesses rather than consumers, information such as vertical industry, number of employees, and company revenues is important.
- *Customer Segmentation.* The objective is to identify logical, unique groups of customers that have similar characteristics and demonstrate similar behaviors relative to the purchase and use of your products. While the promise of "one-to-one marketing" sounds appealing, identification and differentiation of customer segments is a practical place to start.
- *Primary Research.* This effort is undertaken to understand customer needs and attitudes relative to your products, services, and organization as a whole.
- *Customer Valuation.* You must quantify how and how much each customer group contributes to your organization's current profitability as well as future potential value.

This understanding should become increasingly rich and increasingly useful as you continue to interact with your customers.

Develop and Customize

In the product-oriented twentieth century, manufacturers developed products and services and defined distribution networks, then searched for customers. Just think of all of the product failures and short-lived successes that this model has created.

In the customer-focused twenty-first century, product and channel development has to follow the customer's lead. This is the primary basis for competition and competitive differentiation today. Organizations are therefore increasingly developing products and services and customizing communications media and delivery channels based on customer needs and service expectations. Consider the drastic changes in:

- Financial services, where the conveniences of ATMs and electronic banking channels benefit the financial services provider as well as the customer
- Travel, where Web, toll-free phone, and wireless-based reservations and electronic ticketing have offered customers greater flexibility as well as reduced bottlenecks and provider costs
- Business-to-business suppliers of everything from office supplies to temporary help, where online procurement systems allow a business to place just-in-time orders for core products or services

These customer-driven changes in core operating models will continue to reshape our economy.

Interact and Deliver

Interaction is also a critical component of any CRM initiative. Interactive, interaction, interactivity—these are overused terms in today's electronic world, so it is important to define what we mean by interaction.

For many the word *interactive* has become synonymous with "electronic" or "online." However, we cannot lose sight of the two-way reciprocal nature of the term. Most websites today are far less interactive than their offline counterparts. Most offline channels, media, and points of customer contact are far less interactive than they used to be. We have automated most customer touchpoints around *efficiency* rather than interaction. Therefore, our attempts to personalize those automated, mechanized touches that we have with a customer—by acknowledging them by name at the checkout counter or on their return visit to your website—are met with limited enthusiasm by customers.

Remember that interaction does not occur solely through marketing and sales channels. Customers interact in many different ways with many different areas of the organization, ranging from distribution and shipping to customer service to your website. To foster relationships, organizations need to ensure that all areas of the organization:

- Have easy access to relevant, useful customer information. This could range from a customer's product or service preferences to their desired means of receiving communications from your organization.
- Are trained in how to use this customer information in order to tailor their interactions with customers based on both customer needs and potential customer value.

With access to information and appropriate training, organizations will be prepared to steadily increase the value they deliver to customers.

Acquire and Retain

The more you interact with your customers and learn about them, the easier it is to pinpoint those of greatest value to your organization. This insight should drive your acquisition efforts as you attempt to attract those who "look like" your most valuable customers. Your understanding of your most valuable customer segments can make these acquisition efforts increasingly effective, because you can target using the right channel, right media, right product, right offer, right timing, and most relevant message.

Beyond acquisition, successful customer retention involves

getting it "right" on an ongoing basis. Successful retention of your customers is based very simply on the organization's ability to *consistently* deliver on three principles:

1. Maintain interaction; provide an ongoing forum for a two-way dialogue and never stop listening.
2. Continue to deliver on the customer's definition of value.
3. Remember that customers change as they move through different life stages; be alert for the changes and be prepared to modify your service and value proposition as they change.

In keeping with these principles, the CRM cycle continues. As you move from one stage to the next, you gain insight and understanding that enhances your subsequent efforts. Your development initiatives become increasingly sophisticated, as does your implementation of CRM processes and your resulting differentiation in the marketplace.

What Are the Bottom-Line Benefits of CRM?

If you were successful in making customer relationships your primary means of competitive differentiation, what might happen to your bottom line? Imagine these scenarios:

- What if you had more relevant and timely customer information accessible in the call center?
- What if your website was customized to customers' individual interests?
- What if your sales representative understood each organization's procurement process?
- What if your marketing communications were targeted to individual customers' interests and your offers were most relevant to their needs?

While these all sound like wonderful improvements, the trick is to tie them to the bottom line. It may be obvious to you that these and other improvements have an impact on customer acquisition, penetration, retention, and reactivation. It becomes even more obvious that changing these customer metrics can have a major impact on revenues, profitability, and competitive differentiation. Yet unless the relationships between these factors are clearly quantified, the broad impact of CRM across your organization may go unrecognized or understated. Therefore, it is important that you are able to project how your improvements relate directly to your organization's bottom line.

According to Terri Dial, president and CEO of Wells Fargo Bank, "Much of the time, the opening of a new customer account is simply an opportunity to lose money. Most single-account households are unprofitable. We have to build a relationship to make a profit. If we can build a relationship, then we can keep a customer. If we keep customers through relationship building—and not product pushing—they will reward us by buying more, buying profitably, and keeping more of their money with us." Dial's understanding of customer relationship management is definitely a key to this top-tier financial services organization's success.

The bottom line is that CRM initiatives can affect all aspects of provider behavior and related customer behavior. Costs can be reduced and revenues increased. If your efforts can influence even a single behavior or customer-related metric, the payback can be enormous. Your investments in CRM initiatives will result in exponential returns, provided that they are executed well.

Consider the cost of not implementing CRM. Consider the gradual or rapid exodus of your customers. . . . Can you really afford not to implement CRM?

CHAPTER TWO

WHY NOW? WHY ME?

If CRM is such a wonderful concept, why haven't we thought of it sooner? Is it really anything new? What makes CRM appropriate for today's environment? Does CRM make sense for your organization?

Why CRM Now?

Customer relationship management is suddenly the talk of the town. But is CRM simply a new buzzword for something we have always known? Could it be that most major corporations were previously apathetic about their relationships with customers?

If you take a close look, you will recognize that CRM combines the tried-and-true principles of customer satisfaction with new thinking on implementation within the complexities of today's multichannel, multimedia, stratified customer environment. CRM thinking may not be new for customer-focused organizations, but CRM practices—or putting good intentions to action on an increasingly large-scale yet customized basis—is new. For organizations that have not previously embraced customer-focused principles, CRM represents an ever-greater departure from the norm.

CRM has gained widespread popularity in the business community for several reasons. One of the most notable reasons relates to an organization's need to differentiate itself in a highly competitive marketplace. Other reasons include heightened customer expectations and technology enablement.

Competitive Differentiation

CRM promises competitive differentiation in a parity environment where product, price, promotion strategies, and distribution channels are less influential as differentiators than they once were. For example:

- *Product.* Organizations today find it increasingly difficult if not impossible to compete on the basis of product. Technology advancements have enabled the nearly immediate replication of product features and functions. It is just a matter of weeks between a new product launch and the saturation of the market. Just think about it: Are there many products in the marketplace that are truly unique?

- *Price.* Traditionally price has been another basis of competitive differentiation, yet for many companies today, price competition has done nothing more than drive down both the top line and bottom line. Complex channel agreements have furthered parity pricing.

> *"Customer relationships are at the core of our business. It all starts and ends with the customer relationship. Products, channels, and other parts of the business that are currently at the forefront are really subsets and components of what we do with the customer. But the relationship is the crux of [our existence]. Given that we have such an important role to play in the life of the customer, and given that we have so many interactions with the customer, there is a great opportunity to embrace CRM for mutual benefit."*
>
> —Milton Pedraza,
> vice president of CRM
> for Citibank/Latin America

- *Promotion Strategies.* Promotions are extremely easy to readily match. Clubs and points-based programs abound; special offers are the norm; discounts and sales are expected.
- *Place of Distribution.* The Internet and the related advent of e-business have created an avenue for even the smallest businesses to compete. While gaining retail distribution and "shelf space" may still be important, affordable channel alternatives are now more readily available.

While all of these factors are still important, none of them can alone support the success of most businesses. Sheryl Gatto, vice president of consumer marketing at iChoose, an online e-commerce enabler, echoes this thought, stating that " . . . very few things purchased these days are unique; most are commodities with different wrapping paper. The primary difference between two companies is the relationship with the customer." iChoose.com helps consumers save money while they shop online by providing compelling offers on exactly the products they want to purchase. According to Gatto, " . . . Through our software, consumers can configure exactly when [they want us] to notify them of better deals."

Obviously, this business model hinges on customer relationships. CRM—the ability to provide a more meaningful shopping and service experience and therein win customer loyalty—promises to be a means of differentiating; of providing customers with a reason to frequent your business rather than that of your competitors. Ownership of customer relationships and the resulting customer differential provides exponentially greater rewards than differences in product, price, promotion, or place of distribution could ever offer. Weaknesses in these areas may even be mitigated if you can serve as the one-stop provider that can identify, quantify, and then service customers' needs.

Consider the difference between a large membership association such as Automobile Club (AAA) of Southern California with more than six million members and many other product and service providers in this market. An association such as this owns member relationships and has expanded to offer a wide range of qualified products and services—from insurance to travel and financial services—through a wide range of channels—from branch offices to sales agents to the Web—to meet its members' needs. Members benefit from the Automobile Club of Southern California's ability to continually provide value through relevant communications, services, support, and marketing opportunities. According to Jerry Hawkins, group manager, "CRM is simply what our members expect."

This principle of competitive differentiation through customer relationships can be applied in any business model. Take a look at a newspaper publisher whose traditional product, the hardcopy paper, may be declining in readership. Its online news offerings may face intense worldwide competition never experienced in the hardcopy world. The success of the business depends on this publisher's ability to:

- *Recognize the value and the vast potential of its current customer relationships.* Newspapers tend to be tied quite closely to their readers; readers tend to view their papers as relatively trustworthy providers. Are there many other businesses that can claim to have 50–80 percent penetration in a market, which may represent millions of households?
- *Identify additional opportunities to meet customers' needs.* Newspapers have traditionally served as information brokers and also advertising brokers, but primarily within the limitations of their hardcopy product. Looking more broadly at the information broker concept, newspaper publishers could serve as more customized providers of information across a wider range of media and delivery channels. Extending beyond information, newspapers could use their customer understanding to also meet other needs.

Some might caution that such a business should "stick to its knitting," only providing those products/services that they know best. But if what an organization knows best is its customers, its extensibility is greatly increased.

The same concept applies to providers across a wide range of industries. Those that will succeed are those that specialize in customer intelligence and relationships, as well as potentially in the products that they may manufacture or distribute. Very significant customer-focused business models are now being formed in the online world by relationship-driven portals, services, and stores. The "one-stop shop" is close to becoming a reality as sites compete for customers. The success of these initiatives clearly depends on their ability to continually monitor and understand customers' needs, and then to match those needs to relevant products and services in a cost-effective manner. Customer-centric business models trump product-centric models in today's environment.

Heightened Customer Expectations

Another reason CRM has gained popularity relates to the heightened expectations of customers in general. As customers, we are always searching for a better value. That value may be better because of the product, its price, its promotion, or where it can now be purchased. Service, however, is increasingly guiding customer preferences. As service providers begin to compete in this environment, exceptional service becomes the norm, and the bar is raised for all providers. Customer expectations in turn are heightened, and prove difficult if not impossible to lower.

> *". . . Online consumers rule. Their preferences, interests, and needs change rapidly, and to succeed you have to give them what they want."*
>
> —Kim Martin, Director of Customer Relationship Marketing, iChoose

Just think of our expectations today versus ten years ago when it comes to:

- Cellular phone offerings, reliability, and related services
- Health club membership offerings
- Toll-free customer service lines
- Travel reservations
- Credit card products and services
- Securities tracking and trading

Can you imagine turning the clock back and reverting to your life as a customer ten or twenty years ago?

According to Ann Busquet, president of American Express Relationship Services, "Many people believe that we have entered the age of the Internet. Actually, it's more accurate to say that we're living in the age of the customer." Make no mistake: Customers are in control today. They have access to more information than ever before, and they can retrieve it faster than ever before. There has never been a better time to be a customer—or a more demanding time to be a company.

The first challenge of the twenty-first century is to master the changes that come with customers being in control. Companies need to find ways to get to market at lightning speed, to make decisions in real time, and to offer highly personalized products. Each company needs to develop an unprecedented degree of flexibility in order to offer customers what they want, when and how they want it. Companies that manage this transition effectively will thrive; those that don't will fail."

Of course, companies don't change unless the people in them change. It's up to every one of us to figure out how prepared we are to enter the age of the customer. Am I genuinely passionate about doing what's best for customers as opposed to what's easiest for me? Am I willing to surrender a certain amount of control in order to give more control to customers?

These heightened customer expectations drive aggressive marketers to even greater lengths of service. And as Figure 2-1 suggests, the cycle continues. Needless to say, CRM becomes a necessary means of competing in today's customer-driven business environment.

Technology Enablement

Why CRM now? A third important change factor is technology. Ongoing advancements in call center, sales automation, marketing, and online technology have made many of our best intentions and ideas not only feasible but also cost-effective. While the thinking behind CRM may not be new, for most organizations the ability to turn those ideas into action is new.

Granted, we still have a long way to go in terms of automating CRM principles, but we have come a long way. Just five years ago:

- Most large customer databases were proprietary, mainframe-based systems.
- There were no campaign management tools on the marketplace.
- Most call centers maintained proprietary, custom applications.
- Sales force automation applications were limited to electronic Rolodex® functionality.
- Web customization tools and e-mail generation/distribution applications did not exist.

Figure 2-1. Customer expectations driven by CRM.

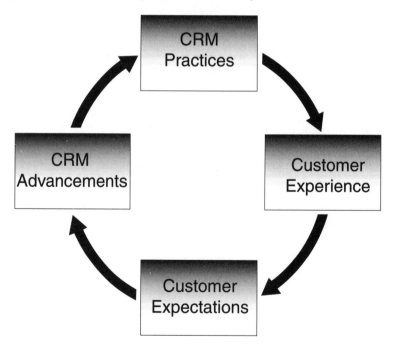

Needless to say, some of these applications are still in their infancy, and we can expect some of them will become integrated components of a CRM solution in the future. Chapter 8 addresses developments in CRM technology that are converging into an integrated solution. While the current CRM systems environment may be less than optimal, technology is already enabling us to interact more appropriately with customers.

Thus, these three factors—competitive differentiation, heightened customer expectations, and technology—explain today's focus on the customer and on CRM.

Why My Organization?

We have established that CRM is appropriate for today's business environment and is enabled by today's technologies.

For some, however, the question still remains, is CRM right for our organization? What if we are successful without it? Does CRM really make sense for everyone? Let's look a little further at the three reasons provided in this chapter:

Reason 1: Competitive differentiation suggests that it is difficult to compete in the business world on any other basis. Product, price, promotion strategies, and place of distribution can all be matched or bettered by competitors. In some industries where the price of entry is high, you may have the upper hand on one of these factors for some period of time, but will be vulnerable to the innovations of competitors at all times. Someone will come along and not just match but better your offering. As a business strategy untapped by most, CRM promises competitive differentiation.

Reason 2: Heightened customer expectations are also difficult to ignore. Our innovations quickly become the norm, and the bar continues to be raised for those who seek to compete. Those who maintain the status quo will find that they are increasingly disappointing their customers, as well as failing to attract new customers.

Reason 3: Enabling technologies such as Internet access tools, data repositories, data mining tools, analysis engines, and terabyte storage make it increasingly feasible to implement CRM. Systems today enable us to market, to sell, and to service much more effectively than we can even imagine. With technology advancements, CRM systems are accessible and used by an increasingly broad range of organizations. Those that do not develop new CRM sales, service, and marketing capabilities will fall behind their competitors' efforts and their customers' related expectations.

For these reasons, I would suggest that CRM makes sense for any organization that has one or more than one customer. The CRM strategies and tactics you employ will be very different if you have one customer or one million, but the principle of focusing on customers and optimizing their relationships with your organization remains the key to your success in today's business climate.

Focus: Ford Motor Company Focuses on Customers

Ford Motor Company is using the Internet as its means of understanding its customers. Not unlike many other manufacturers, traditionally the automaker's dealer channels have kept it one (if not two) steps removed from understanding who its customers were and what they wanted. Ford has launched an e-business strategy that includes:

- A Buyer Connection website, where consumers can order custom-assembled cars, track their progress, and apply for financing
- An Owner Connection website, where owners can access online help, manage their warranty service, and monitor financing

- A research and analysis ability to monitor the interests and buying patterns of web-surfing customers

According to Ford design chief J. Mays, "This [strategy] gives us a bird's-eye view of what consumers want out of a car before we build it." These capabilities also allow Ford to provide increased service and support, and gain significant competitive differentiation.

CHAPTER THREE

It's All about the Customer Experience

As suggested in the first two chapters, experienced customers are in the driver's seat, expecting increasingly valuable experiences from their providers. CRM can only provide your organization with the customer differential if you have won the loyalty and advocacy of your customers. In that respect, CRM is all about the customer experience.

While this sounds like a fairly straightforward concept, consistently optimizing each customer's experience with your organization is no small undertaking. There are several critical aspects of your organization that impact the customer's experience. The Customer Experience Cycle (see Figure 3-1) provides an overview of what is involved.

Customer Understanding

This cycle begins in the center—the customer experience begins with the customer. Assessing the customer experience must begin

Figure 3-1. Customer Experience Cycle (detailed view).

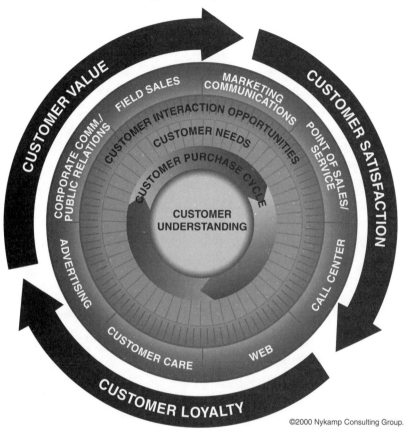

©2000 Nykamp Consulting Group.

with an understanding of unique customer groups and their related characteristics and behaviors. A customer's experience with you and their perceptions of your organization, and your ability to implement CRM strategies, will vary depending on who those customers are. For example, are your customers individuals within households, or does the household form a buying entity? There are other variables as well:

- Are your customers primarily businesses? If so, who within the business influences the purchase? Who initiates the purchase?

- What are your customers' buying characteristics and preferences?
- What is the history of your relationship with each customer?
- How do they prefer to interact with you?
- What are their purchase and related spending patterns? What is their current and potential value to your organization?
- Which of their needs are you currently fulfilling? Which needs are you not fulfilling today? Who is fulfilling those needs?
- Why did your customers choose you over your competitors? How do your customers differ from your competitors' customers?
- What are your customers' overall satisfaction levels with various aspects of your organization and offerings? What are their expectations?
- Based on these factors, how many unique segments of customers do you have? What are the critical differentiators?
- Which customer segments are most valuable to your organization, and why?

Answers to these and many other questions drive all of your CRM investments and strategies. Addressing these essential issues, however, takes significant time and effort because this information is rarely readily available. Ongoing data collection efforts should be pursued as a means of populating and maintaining key customer information. Customer profiling and segmentation efforts will then provide a continued means of monitoring the composition of your customer base and the characteristics of unique customer segments. These efforts are addressed further in subsequent chapters.

Needless to say, this initial customer understanding is the basis for evaluating the customer experience with your organization. More broadly speaking, this customer understanding provides the foundation for all of your CRM efforts.

Customer Purchase Cycle

Once unique customer segments are established and the profiles of each segment are understood, the next step involves defining the unique purchase cycles of each segment, relative to your products and/or services. Specifically, you want to define:

- *The Stages of the Purchase Cycle.* For low-involvement products, this may equate to three to four simple stages such as awareness, decision making, purchase, and consumption. For high-involvement products, such as technology products, there may be six to eight stages with significant evaluation, installation, and training effort stages of the process.

- *The Length of Each Stage.* This may vary significantly by customer segment: For some customers, the purchase of airline tickets may take a matter of minutes; for others, the same purchase may require weeks of time.

- *The Related Complexity of Each Stage.* For high-involvement products, the decision-making stage may take months, if not years. For low-involvement products, a decision may be made in a matter of seconds.

- *The Indicators of When a Customer Enters a Stage.* These indicators may equate to the channels they use, the questions they ask, the information they request, or any combination of behaviors. It is critical to understand the signals that indicate where the customer is in the purchase process. Are they really "just looking" or are they ready to buy?

- *The Frequency at which a Customer Repeats the Cycle.* It could be weekly for consumable products and services; it could be once in ten years for equipment or appliances.

- *The Level of Resources Directed at Each Stage.* It is important to understand where your organization is currently investing time and attention; where you are focusing your efforts today.

All of these factors vary tremendously by product category and by customer characteristics. The purchase cycle for automobiles may require several months; the purchase cycle for most packaged goods involves just moments of time.

Advances in technology have an increasingly major impact on customer purchase cycles. In some cases, new channels and new media have abbreviated the purchase process. E-commerce sites, for example, have enabled consumers to very efficiently compare and contrast alternative products and initiate a purchase, twenty-four hours a day; seven days a week. In other cases, new technology solutions have actually elongated and increased the complexity of the purchase process. Online information portals, for example, seek to educate consumers; online auctions and order consolidation websites focus on price bidding or savings over time.

Defining these segment-specific purchase cycles typically involves a combination of quantitative and qualitative research. Quantitative research can often be driven from the history of customer interactions that your organization may be maintaining in a customer database. Qualitative research, on the other hand, may involve interviews or other in-depth discussions of customer behavior. Understanding these purchase cycles is critical in defining and then acting on relevant experiences.

Customer Needs

Each customer has unique needs at each stage of the purchase cycle. These needs may relate to information, convenience, efficiency, price, reputation, and/or a variety of other issues. For example, a frequent traveler who commutes weekly between New York and Denver would have a high need for convenience through all aspects of the ticketing and flight process. Information needs related to flight schedules, carry-on restrictions, refund policies, and other details would be minimal. For the infrequent traveler between these two cities, information needs may be extremely high throughout the process, and convenience may be sacrificed for price. It is critical to understand how these needs vary by customer segment, and how these needs change as a customer progresses through the purchase cycle. For a business customer, you will need to understand both the needs of the business and the needs of the individual involved in the purchase process. The business's needs may relate to the function, reliability, and price of the product. The individual's needs may relate to the reputation of the product, provider, and the support that will be provided with the product. Understanding both organizational and individual needs is critical to furthering a purchase process.

Defining these needs also involves a combination of quantitative and qualitative research that could be conducted in conjunction with the definition of purchase cycles outlined previously.

Customer Interaction Opportunities

Finally, each customer's unique purchase cycle, needs, characteristics, and behaviors present a wide range of customer interaction opportunities. These opportunities are:

- *Tied to specific stages of the purchase cycle.* Your opportunities to communicate product features and benefits to a customer are significantly different when a customer is in a passive awareness mode compared to when a customer is actively making a purchase decision. Your opportunities to provide site personalization and customized service are much greater as your relationship with a customer strengthens.

- *Inbound and outbound.* Some interactions, such as a call to customer service or a visit to your website, are initiated by the customer. Others, such as outbound marketing communications and sales efforts, are initiated by you as the provider.

- *Cross-channel and cross-media.* You may find that specific types of interactions lend themselves to direct channels and media; others may lend themselves to an indirect information-serving environment.

- *Situation-driven or driven by a deeper understanding of customer needs and behaviors.* An example would include sending information to prospective customers based on their request for information. An example of the latter would be recognizing a customer's channel and media preferences and driving marketing efforts accordingly.

You should be able to itemize dozens, if not hundreds, of opportunities to interact. Figure 3-2 provides some thought-starters by itemizing some of the potential areas of customer contact with your organization. Some of these customer interaction opportunities will obviously be more important than others. Therefore, it is critical to assess each of them based on:

- Their impact on customer satisfaction and value and on customer relationships
- Feasibility of implementation, and the extent of development work that would be required for improving each interaction
- Related priority for development or improvement

Figure 3-2. Potential points of customer contact.

Sales	**Staff Functions**
Telesales—Inbound	Accounts Receivable
Telesales—Outbound	Credit Department
Point of Service/Sale	Collections
Field Sales	Billing
Store Personnel	
Layaway Department	**Marketing Communications**
	Customer Acquisition
Customer Service/Support	Customer Retention
Customer Service	Customer Reactivation
Customer Training	General Advertising
Customer Support	Public Relations
Voice Recognition Unit (VRU)	
Website Support	
Service/Repair Department	
Claims	
Warranty Department	
Distribution	
Delivery Personnel	
"Will Call" Window	
Order Processing	
Shipping/Fulfillment	

The sum total of these interactions—those supported as well as those not supported today—form the customer's experience with your organization. You may find that this experience is very positive for some of your customer segments, but less positive for others. This could be based on their needs, behaviors, and preferences. Once you realize the extent to which you support and enhance a customer's experience, you can put a game plan in place to adjust your efforts accordingly.

As shown in Figure 3-1, the customer's experience across all aspects of your organization—whether it's field sales, marketing, point-of-sale, call center, website, customer care, advertising, or public relations—drives customer satisfaction. Customer satisfaction can foster loyalty; in turn a customer's loyalty forms the basis of a valuable relationship with your organization.

Focus: Dell Computer and the Customer Experience Council

Dell is convinced that the customer experience is key to its current and future success, and this philosophy is reflected in Dell's mission: "to be the most successful computer company in the world at delivering the best customer experience in markets we serve."

Building a great company on the Web isn't about "aggregating eyeballs," "increasing stickiness," or embracing any of the other slogans that masquerade as strategy. It's about rethinking the most basic relationship in business: the one between you and your customers. How well do you meet their needs? How smoothly do you solve their problems? How quickly do you anticipate what they'll want next? The real promise of the Web is a once-and-for-all transfer of power: Consumers and business customers will get what they want—when and how they want it, and even at the price they want. Jerry Gregoire, chief information officer at Dell, puts it this way: "The customer experience is the next competitive battleground."

How does the dominant maker of personal computers in the industry define the customer experience? "It's the sum total of the interactions that a customer has with a company's products, people, and processes," says Richard Owen, vice president of Dell online worldwide. "It goes from the moment when customers see an ad to the moment when they accept delivery of a product—and beyond. Sure, we want people to think that our computers are great. But what matters is the totality of customers' experiences with us: talking with our call center representatives, visiting our website, buying a PC, owning a PC. The customer experience reflects all of those interactions."

The company formed the Customer Experience Council, a group that is scrutinizing every aspect of how Dell interacts with customers. By Dell's reckoning, the company has more than 16 million "customer contacts" per week, whether in the form of e-mails, phone calls, deliveries, or returns. The challenge: how to monitor and measure the quality of those contacts.

"Every public company tells shareholders how it's doing every quarter," says Paul Bell, senior vice president for Dell's home and small-business group, who is a member of the Customer Experience Council. "But few companies have a set of metrics that measure the customer experience month to month, quarter to quarter.

"Our challenge is to instill a companywide commitment to the customer experience," he continues. "It's like the way Disney teaches its people to be aggressively friendly: 'Can I help you find something?' Our metrics give us a read on the experience that we're delivering and on the loyalty that we're creating. We're doing pretty well, but . . . know we can do much better."

CHAPTER FOUR

THE CRM TRANSFORMATION PROCESS

We have addressed how customer relationship management equates to a customer differential and significant competitive advantage. We have also addressed what effective CRM looks like from a customer's perspective. However, the enterprisewide nature and broad reach of CRM can be a daunting proposition for any organization to even begin to undertake.

Several key aspects of your organization will need to undergo significant change in order to support and foster CRM initiatives. The CRM Business Transformation Map in Figure 4-1 illustrates the five interrelated aspects of change:

1. Business focus
2. Organizational structure
3. Business metrics
4. Customer interaction
5. Technology

Figure 4-1. CRM Transformation Map.

B U S I N E S S F O C U S					
Products	Sales	Channels	Marketing	Services	Customers

O R G A N I Z A T I O N A L S T R U C T U R E					
Product Management	Place Management	Promotion Management	Channel Management	Contact Management	Customer Management

B U S I N E S S M E T R I C S					
Product Performance	Place Performance	Program Performance	Customer Revenues	Customer Satisfaction	Customer Lifetime Value and Loyalty

C U S T O M E R I N T E R A C T I O N					
Mass Transaction	Opportunistic Promotion	Targeted Campaigns	Segment-Specific Communication	Customer-Contact Integration	Individual Permission-Based Interaction

T E C H N O L O G Y					
Transaction Processing	Data Maintenance	Data Access	Data Maintenance	Data Marts	Customer Touchpoint Systems

©1999 Nykamp Consulting Group.

The map depicts typical stages of transformation within established organizations. The stages of transformation are shown from left to right, from the more traditional product or transaction orientation to the optimal customer-focused orientation. It is important to note that:

- Becoming a customer-centric organization is truly a transformation that involves tremendous change. It is not an evolution; it is not a gradual shift and does not happen naturally.
- The transformation does not involve incremental steps, from left to right, on the map. The further you are from the right-hand side, the greater the leap you need to make.
- These stages are not mutually exclusive; progression does not entail abandoning any previous stage. Rather, it is a matter of shifting resources and emphasis.

Business Focus Transformation

Transforming the business focus of an organization essentially equates to an organization's adoption of the customer-focused

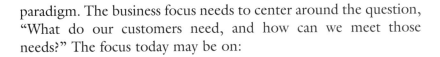

paradigm. The business focus needs to center around the question, "What do our customers need, and how can we meet those needs?" The focus today may be on:

- *Products.* The organization may focus on how it can make a better widget or otherwise expand its product line.
- *Sales.* The organization may focus heavily on the sales channel, and overemphasize the importance of having "feet on the street" as the key to its success.
- *Channels.* Likewise, the organization may put its channel strategy—that is, management of multiple channels—above all else.
- *Marketing.* While a marketing focus may seem to be a step in the right direction, many organizations become trapped in marketing tactics; the focus is on the marketing rather than the customer.
- *Service.* As with marketing, a focus on service is certainly intuitive and can benefit customers greatly. However, a focus on service can lead to very operational, tactical thinking, and cloud the bigger picture.

This business focus transformation—focusing on customers—is critical to the success of any CRM initiative. If the organization only takes a secondary or tertiary interest in its customers, its CRM efforts are guaranteed to fall short if not fail.

Organizational Structure Transformation
Changing the organizational structure of a company goes hand-in-hand with the change in business focus. Most organizations today are organized around:

- *Products*, with product managers driving business decisions.
- *Places*, with regional, branch, or store-specific management structures.
- *Promotions*, with departments responsible for specific media or marketing efforts. This model is particularly common in direct marketing businesses.

- *Channels*, with retail, e-commerce, and/or other specific channel structures.
- *Contacts*, with the business organized around functional interactions with customers. There may be customer acquisition, cross-sell, retention, and reactivation departments.

The transformation to a *customer-focused* organization should lead to a management structure that's organized around your customers, with teams responsible for all interactions with different segments of customers. This is a major hurdle for most organizations, because it often means augmenting the existing product or channel structure with customer management staff and additional headcount.

Business Metrics Transformation

Transforming the organization's business metrics is a by-product of the changes that result from the business focus and organizational structure changes. Therefore, the transformation progresses as follows:

- Focusing on *product* performance is the most natural first step, in keeping with a product-focused organization with product management structures.
- *Place* performance essentially equates to measures and comparisons of productivity and profitability across regions or territories.
- *Program* performance is the focus of many marketing and sales groups, with measures of productivity and profitability tied to each campaign.
- The emphasis may shift to *customer revenues*, meaning the immediate-term productivity of each customer.
- *Customer satisfaction* measurement equates to rudimentary monitoring of the customer experience.

The final stage—*customer lifetime value and loyalty*—transfers your primary focus to the ultimate question of customer

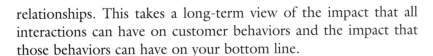

relationships. This takes a long-term view of the impact that all interactions can have on customer behaviors and the impact that those behaviors can have on your bottom line.

Customer Interaction Transformation

Transforming the nature of your customer interactions can only take place with the participation of all who are responsible for inbound and outbound contacts. Moving to individual-based interactions is a big leap for most organizations that today may have a focus on:

- *Mass Transactions.* The focus is on the completion of a transaction—at the checkout counter, over the phone, or through the e-commerce site—rather than the formation of customer relationships.

- *Opportunistic Promotions.* The organization provides special offers based on business needs rather than customer needs.

- *Targeted Campaigns.* The focus is on the performance of each marketing effort rather than the performance of customers.

- *Segment-Specific Communications.* The organization centers its efforts on developing appropriate streams of outbound communications for a customer segment.

- *Customer Contact Integration.* The focus is on the coordination and consistency of customer contacts across media, channels, and products.

Again, these strategies are not inappropriate. Targeting customer segments based on business opportunities and contact strategies makes inherently good sense. However, the greater opportunity is in moving toward a two-way interaction strategy that is *individual-based* rather than segment-based, and that is driven from an *ongoing dialogue* with customers, in which both parties have expressed a willingness and interest in interaction. This requires an increasingly large investment of time and resources, but promises exponential rewards.

Technology Transformation

Finally, there is an essential technology transformation. CRM technology must support and enable meaningful customer dialogue at all points of contact. The shift of resources and emphasis usually progresses as follows:

- The essential initial focus of most organizations is on systems that support the *processing of transactions* in an operational environment.
- *Data maintenance* is a second early stage that focuses on simply storing the data that has been processed.
- A focus on *data access* reflects an early need of most organizations for basic reporting capabilities and also the basic movement of data within the organization.
- The *data warehouse* emphasis is on the centralization of data from across many areas of the organization.
- The related *data mart* focus has been on the creation of practical, subject-oriented subsets of data to drive specific business applications.

The emphasis on *customer touchpoint systems* combines the concepts of operational transaction on processing with data-driven decision making. Having the right customer information at each point of contact supports an increasingly relevant and valuable customer experience. CRM technology has received a great deal of attention in the vendor community, because it seems that most everyone has a system to sell. Technology is actually the easiest of the areas to change . . . you can "buy your way" over to the right-hand side of the Transformation Map and purchase integrated customer touchpoint systems. Because off-the-shelf or hosted CRM software solutions are readily available in the marketplace, technology often gets ahead of the other areas of transformation. Technology plays a critical support role, but should not be the driver of CRM initiatives.

In summary, all five aspects of the organization need to change and in some shape or form become customer-centric, in order to effectively support CRM. Four out of five—or some other fractional level of participation—will not work. Remember that you will only be as strong as your weakest link.

CRM is therefore a broad business concept that has far-reaching implications across your organization. To move forward, we recommend that you first identify where your organization is today in each of these five areas, and then develop a phased plan for change. Ultimately, success is based on organizational readiness: your ability and willingness to change.

This book's remaining chapters provide you with the specifics on each of these areas of transformation, planning processes for transformation within your organization, and means of measuring your success. In addition, there are examples of how a very diverse group of organizations is implementing CRM.

Focus: Reaching through the Channel at HP

According to Roger Williams of Hewlett-Packard, "Large amounts of HP's business goes through the channel— retail for consumer products; resellers for PCs and printers; and original equipment manufacturers (OEMs), value-added resellers (VARs), independent software vendors (ISVs), and application service providers (ASPs) for high-end servers. Establishing and maintaining relationships with the end-customer is not easy in these situations, but HP considers it essential to do so.

"For example, in its consumer business, HP is investing heavily in CRM solutions to reach customers. Customers are identified from product registrations, and e-mail newsletters are used to maintain contact with them. Web communities are another tool used to provide valuable information to customers (e.g., on home-printing ideas and applications). Internet-based relationship building is a cost-effective way to reach low-dollar-value but still important customers. However, in order to sustain the relationship, HP is conscious of the need to actively manage the frequency of contact and respect customers' wishes and privacy."

CHAPTER FIVE

CRM IMPLEMENTATION

The customer experience work outlined in Chapter 3 and the CRM transformation process outlined in Chapter 4 together provide the conceptual framework for getting started . . . for beginning to implement or improve customer relationship management practices within your organization.

Successful implementation of CRM requires the development of a highly detailed and comprehensive action plan. As with any critical organizational initiative, planning is the key to success. This is especially true with an initiative such as CRM that affects the entire enterprise. Planning for CRM is important because it will help you develop:

- A common set of CRM business goals related to increased revenues, decreased costs, and competitive differentiation
- Uniform strategies for reaching those goals

- Infrastructure plans for successful implementation
- Measures of success to monitor your progress and to quantify your achievements

On the basis of my experience assisting a wide range of complex organizations in CRM planning, I am recommending a simple yet very systematic approach. The essential steps should include:

1. *Situation Assessment.* Where does our organization currently stand?
2. *CRM Gap Analysis.* What are the gaps that need to be closed in order to effectively implement CRM?
3. *Action Plan.* How should we stage our efforts to ensure that our investments are tied to short-term and longer-term deliverables?

Your organization should form an internal multidisciplinary transformation team for the initial and ongoing CRM planning and management. All key areas of the organization should be represented within this team. All team members need to dedicate significant time and effort to make this approach work.

While an organization can build a CRM action plan on its own, many find that an outside perspective can add a greater measure of objectivity and practicality to the process. In addition, one of the key benefits of the planning process is achieving consensus within the organization about what CRM means, how the organization can benefit, and what the priority and timing of CRM-based activities should be. Because many of these issues are rife with controversy, an outside firm may be best suited to help the organization quickly achieve and maintain consensus.

The remainder of this chapter walks through the three steps of CRM planning and provides guidance for your CRM transformation team and all participants.

Step 1: Situation Assessment

The key to building the CRM action plan is in understanding where your organization stands on CRM issues today. A situation assessment will enable your organization to identify, size, and prioritize current CRM initiatives in your environment. This process alone is often very revealing. This work can best be accomplished through a series of interviews and discussion sessions with senior executives, managers, and staff. Discussions with key individuals across departments may identify that there are ten, twenty, or even thirty divergent CRM initiatives being pursued. While all of these initiatives may have merit, failure to understand dependencies and to prioritize efforts based on value can lead to significant challenges.

It will not be unusual to find a wide variety of goals and objectives for CRM across the different areas of your organization. Some will have a broad vision of what CRM can mean, while others will have a relatively limited view. This initial assessment is necessary to help you define a CRM vision and mission for the entire organization.

There are two essential aspects of a CRM situation assessment; the first being an internal evaluation of your capabilities, and the second being an external assessment of the customer's experience with your organization.

Internal Evaluation

The situation assessment should involve an internal evaluation of your CRM capabilities and infrastructure. The result should be a detailed assessment and resultant mapping of your organization in the five business areas outlined in the CRM Transformation Map, which was first discussed in Chapter 4 and is repeated here in Figure 5-1.

It is essential in the situation assessment to gain consensus on this internal evaluation because it reveals where your organization is today and what your current strengths and weaknesses are in each of these areas. This common understanding will provide a basis for your strategies and your allocation of resources and related investments. Involve representatives from various areas of your

Figure 5-1. CRM Transformation Map.

BUSINESS FOCUS					
Products	Sales	Channels	Marketing	Services	Customers

ORGANIZATIONAL STRUCTURE					
Product Management	Place Management	Promotion Management	Channel Management	Contact Management	Customer Management

BUSINESS METRICS					
Product Performance	Place Performance	Program Performance	Customer Revenues	Customer Satisfaction	Customer Lifetime Value and Loyalty

CUSTOMER INTERACTION					
Mass Transaction	Opportunistic Promotion	Targeted Campaigns	Segment-Specific Communication	Customer-Contact Integration	Individual Permission-Based Interaction

TECHNOLOGY					
Transaction Processing	Data Maintenance	Data Access	Data Maintenance	Data Marts	Customer Touchpoint Systems

©1999 Nykamp Consulting Group.

organization in this exercise, and discuss similarities and differences of opinions. Determine the most representative depiction of your organization. Gaining consensus on this map in the beginning of the process is important, too, because it will be used as an ongoing tool for measuring your success, as described in Chapter 11.

External Evaluation

The second aspect of a CRM situation assessment is an external assessment of the customers' experience with your organization. The concept of a Customer Experience Cycle, as outlined in Chapter 3 and shown in Figure 5-2, can serve as your tool for this work.

Assessing the customer's experience with your organization involves:

- Determining whether to analyze the experience of your customers as a whole, or key groups.

Figure 5-2. Customer experience cycle.

©2000 Nykamp Consulting Group.

- Utilizing a combination of primary and secondary, quantitative and qualitative research to understand the characteristics, needs, and interaction opportunities throughout their purchase cycle. Most organizations will have some existing research to provide a baseline understanding. It is obviously important not to rely on preconceived notions about who your customers are and how they interact. You may be aware of the expectations rather than the norm, and therefore need to take an objective look at what your customers are really all about.

- Prioritizing interaction opportunities based on impact and ability to implement. Your organization needs to agree on how to invest in CRM—which systems, touchpoints, or related processes to improve. Realistically speaking, you will not be able to optimize every touchpoint; decisions need to be made regarding the "touches" that deserve your time and attention.

Step 2: CRM Gap Analysis

The second step in the CRM planning process should be a gap analysis. This analysis is essentially a comparison between an organization's current state and the desired state. The internal and external evaluation work conducted in step 1 should provide the basis for this evaluation. The external evaluation work in step 1 results in a prioritized list of interaction opportunities. For all high-priority opportunities, it is essential to define the desired customer experience. This involves spelling out the step-by-step processes that should take place at the critical customer interaction points:

- What should happen when one of your best customers calls to complain about a billing problem?
- What should happen when a prospective customer registers on your website and requests additional information?
- What should happen when the account executive for one of your largest clients leaves the company?
- What should happen when a customer calls customer service three times within ten days?
- What should happen when a customer does not renew a policy, or allows a subscription to go inactive?
- What should happen when a customer receives an initial sales visit?
- What should happen when a customer attends a training seminar?

Itemize the series of small but important events and processes that need to take place in response to these critical interactions. While some of them seem obvious, gaining agreement on standard practices will enable you to operationalize them.

From an external standpoint, itemizing the activity around each of your high-priority interaction opportunities will highlight gaps in information, systems, and business processes, as well as deficiencies in resources and staffing.

Taking a broader internal look at your organization's capabilities, you can categorize gaps in business focus, organizational structure, business metrics, customer interaction capabilities, and technology.

Gaps in Business Focus

When addressing business focus, companies typically find that the gaps relate to their:

- Definition of the customer
- Knowledge of customer behaviors
- Understanding of customer attitudes, needs, and preferences
- Commitment to satisfying customer needs

While these areas may seem somewhat elementary, they receive limited time and attention in most organizations.

Gaps in Organizational Structure

Organizational gaps address roles and responsibilities, business processes, employee performance measurements, and the related compensation or incentive systems. While these issues may seem a step removed from the customer experience, they can and often do have a tremendous impact on individual and group behavior relative to customers.

Gaps in Business Metrics

Gaps in business metrics are often related to measurement of customer performance on a segment-by-segment basis, such as gaps in customer acquisition, customer development, customer reten-tion, customer migration, and customer reactivation. The gap analysis addresses the ability of the organization to generate and track these metrics on a customer scorecard, as explained further in Chapter 8.

Gaps in Customer Interaction Capabilities

These gaps actually become increasingly apparent by looking at the customers' experience with your organization. Are you able to interact with customers:

- At all points of contact? Do you recognize who they are, and the depth and breadth of their relationship with your organization?
- Across all areas of your organization? Do you appear as one company or many to your customers?
- Across sales, service, and marketing functions?

In short, having a coordinated, cohesive interaction capability is critical to your success.

Gaps in Technology

Technology gaps may relate to:

- Consistent data collection
- Distributing the "right" customer information to each point of contact
- Tracking and trending customer performance over time

These gaps often mistakenly become the focal point of many organizations' CRM efforts because these gaps are in many cases the least controversial to resolve.

Organizational Readiness

In addition to the interaction opportunities and the five dimensions of the CRM transformation map, the gap analysis should also address organizational readiness relative to leadership and resources. Senior management must not only "buy in," but actively endorse and become engaged in the CRM transformation process. Qualified resources must also be committed to all aspects of the work, and roles and responsibilities for leading the transformation must be carefully defined.

Taking a hard look at these areas is absolutely critical to your success. Overstating or overestimating your capabilities in any of these areas will lead to problems down the road. The broad, interdependent nature of CRM requires a breadth of resources and capabilities and a depth of commitment.

The result of step 2 is an itemization of gaps in business processes, capabilities, and infrastructure to support the optimal customer experience and high-priority customer interactions.

Step 3: CRM Action Plan

The gap analysis will likely identify very sizable change initiatives, as well as relatively small-scale tactical improvements in key customer interactions. Prioritization and balancing of these initiatives is critical and should be based on four key criteria:

- *Cost* to implement, including initial one-time costs as well as anticipated ongoing expenses
- *Benefit* in terms of increased revenue, decreased costs, and/or increased competitive differentiation
- *Feasibility* based on organizational readiness, senior management acceptance, resource skill sets and availability, systems support, and a number of other factors
- *Time* required to implement, including the time necessary for training and addressing "cultural" change management issues

This work should drive the development of a very detailed action plan. While the complete plan might span three or more years, it should be divided into six-month phases with clear deliverables that will demonstrate measures of progress and success.

The plan should identify interdependent activities and should comprehensively detail the time and resources required for each activity.

It is critical that you gain the support and commitment of all who will be responsible for implementing, sponsoring, and funding the various aspects of the plan. This will naturally be a very diverse group that may require a number of different communications strategies. However, each person's participation in finalizing the action plan will greatly benefit the actual implementation effort.

A related, critical element is the development of a leadership action plan. Advancing your CRM capabilities requires significant organizational change. The leadership plan should assess the drivers and restraints of this change and the organization's readiness to embrace change. You should highlight specific leadership actions necessary to promote the organizational change. Executives should be able to identify their roles and responsibilities and the actions necessary to eliminate barriers and nurture change.

Continued CRM Implementation

Successful ongoing implementation of CRM requires managing all efforts with detailed project plans, deadlines, and ongoing tracking and measurement. Maintain the Transformation Map (shown in Figure 5-1), which depicts progress across all areas of your organization. Also maintain a scorecard that accounts for more immediate project-based accomplishments. This documentation will enable the organization to capitalize on learnings. The action plan should be reviewed and modified two to four times a year to ensure consistency and relevance. Finally, an organization should recognize that the transformation is never truly "complete." It will be an ongoing process focused on continual improvement.

Changing Your Business Focus

At the heart of any CRM transformation is a change in business focus—from products, sales, channels, marketing, and/or service to customers. This fundamental shift in focus is essential to your CRM success.

Business Focus or Blur?

At the heart of most organizations is a series of interrelated strategies addressing products, services, distribution, markets, resources, and infrastructure. Success today belongs to those who have a fundamental focus on customers driving strategies in each of these areas. For many, the temptation is to retrofit customers into existing plans and processes. The obvious danger in this approach is that existing plans and processes may be far from ideal or may even run contrary to a customer-centric approach.

A business focus on customers, then, equates to an organization:

- Embracing the premise that optimizing customer relationships is the key to future success.

- Supporting the vision of CRM throughout the organization.

- Understanding the widespread impact that CRM may have on business strategies and on all functional areas of the organization.

- Being open to wholesale changes in business strategies in order to truly foster CRM.

- Providing leadership at the highest levels of the organization and the resources necessary to implement this change and to continually refine CRM strategies.

Big Challenge = Big Opportunity

The enterprisewide nature of CRM is both its biggest challenge and its biggest opportunity. This enterprise perspective means that:

- *CRM is not exclusively a marketing initiative.* Many have equated CRM with customer-focused marketing or data-driven marketing. CRM requires marketing expertise and results in more effective, data-driven marketing efforts. However, CRM is not strictly a marketing initiative.

- *CRM is not exclusively a sales initiative.* Many have equated CRM with sales force automation (SFA) and more effective account management. Certainly sales strategies and performance can benefit from a customer-centric approach. CRM requires support of the sales organization. Sales, however, is just one piece of the puzzle.

- *CRM is also not exclusively a service initiative.* As with sales and marketing, customer service is one functional aspect of successful CRM implementation.

- *CRM is not a technology initiative.* Many organizations have assigned all of their CRM efforts to their information services (IS) or information technology (IT) group. Frequently CRM conferences equate to technology exhibits and demonstrations, which gives the impression that an off-the-shelf product can be easily implemented by the IT group alone. Certainly, technology is needed to implement CRM, but technology is not the driver of CRM.

CRM involves marketing, sales, service, and technology as well as other functional areas of your organization. CRM requires all areas of the organization to not only exist in harmony, but to be working together toward the common goal of building stronger customer relationships. Having even one broken spoke in the wheel—one area of the organization that is less than fully committed to CRM—can make the difference between success and failure. The broad nature of CRM is a defining characteristic that cannot be overemphasized.

Minimizing CRM Minimizes Your Success

You might wonder, wouldn't it be easier for everyone involved if one group of an organization were to initially adopt a CRM charter or launch a CRM project, and then broaden its influence over time? The IT group, for example, might begin with a new customer service system or new customer information architecture. Alternatively, marketing might begin with its vision of CRM—a standard customer segmentation scheme and related measures of customer lifetime value. The sales organization might begin with an aggressive account profiling and realignment effort. Any one of these projects would seem to have certain benefits. For example:

- Senior management could more readily approve one of these projects, particularly if the members of senior management represent diverse interests.
- A departmental project would potentially represent less of an investment and therefore less risk than an enterprisewide solution.
- A departmental project could also be more feasible to implement, since the work would remain within one functional area of the organization and would require less collaboration.

It is tempting to launch CRM on a limited basis within one functional area of an organization. Quite frankly, it is how CRM is being pursued by most organizations today. Yet I maintain that any initiative that minimizes the broad-sweeping importance of CRM also minimizes longer-term success. While it is important to start small and to implement change gradually, it is equally important to lay the groundwork for this change and establish the related larger vision for the future before launching any independent initiatives.

The danger is that CRM may otherwise be:

- Viewed as a functional, departmental initiative, both by senior management and by other areas of the organization.
- Limited to short-term initiatives that can be implemented within one area of the organization.
- Limited to the related budgets and resources that would be afforded to a single department and a single initiative.

The moral here is that minimizing CRM to a project, a department, or a function does not serve anyone well. Chapter 7, "Organizing around CRM," discusses this issue of CRM ownership in more detail. Suffice it to say that CRM cannot have a single departmental, functional focus within most organizations.

The Focus of Most Organizations

This focus on customers is all new for even the most progressive organizations. Most organizations today remain focused alternatively on products, sales, channels, marketing, or service (see Figure 6-1).

Figure 6-1. Business focus transformation.

BUSINESS FOCUS					
Products	Sales	Channels	Marketing	Services	Customers

©1999 Nykamp Consulting Group.

Product Focus

Most traditional organizations—particularly manufacturers—are focused heavily if not exclusively on the products that they produce and distribute. Organizations hire product managers, create product divisions and units, and develop product goals and measures. Consider these examples:

- A tool manufacturer may be convinced that a superior product will "sell itself," as long as distribution channels are secured.
- A software company may believe that a better product will unseat a much larger competitor.
- A retailer may believe that having the right lines in the right sizes at the right time is the primary means of optimizing sales.
- A restaurant may be convinced that its soup, bread, or special entree is the key to its success.

Yet in today's marketplace, it is seldom the case that focusing on product alone is your key to success. As addressed in Chapter 2, product is seldom a critical differentiator, and therefore needs to be bundled with other dimensions in order to drive business success.

Sales Focus

Organizations that sell to businesses are typically focused on the effectiveness of their sales channel. They may have their own sales force or work with third-party sales representatives. The overarching business model is to create top-of-mind awareness and then deploy a sales force to push products into the marketplace. Consider these examples:

- A computer hardware manufacturer, facing slumping sales, realigns its sales force and brings in a new vice president of sales.
- A business-to-business telecommunications concern projects quarterly revenues based solely on the assumption of each salesperson reaching his or her quotas.

- A multilevel marketer assumes that enrolling additional layers of sales consultants will effectively increase market share.

- A distributor believes that more extravagant sales promotions will drive incremental volume.

The common denominator in all of these examples is a single-minded focus on sales volume.

For many organizations, a focus on sales also translates to an emphasis on new customer acquisition, which usually means the organization is incurring tremendous costs in finding and attracting new customers. Therefore, while a sales capability is critical to the success of many organizations, it alone cannot drive that success. The critical flaw in most aggressive sales-driven organizations is a lack of focus on ongoing customer relationships.

Channel Focus

Some organizations spend most of their time, energy, and resources on optimizing their channels of distribution. The premise here is that if we have the right store locations or the right dealers carrying our products, or if we launch a new e-commerce channel and minimize channel conflict through effective management strategies, then we will optimize our revenue and profitability.

While continual management and refinement of channel strategies is critical to any business's success, that effort cannot stand alone. Being where the customer can find you is the cost of entry, not the key to your success.

Marketing Focus

Many organizations confuse a marketing focus with a customer focus. There are, however, sizable differences. Organizations with a marketing focus:

- View advertising and marketing strategies, programs, and implementation skill sets as the key to their success. They may not have the best product or the right distribution channels, but the belief is that if they market smarter, these challenges can be overcome.

- May or may not be in tune with customer needs and opportunities.
- Seldom recognize the breadth of the customer's total experience with the organization.
- Seldom have the ability to influence the customer's experience at each touchpoint.
- Measure the success of all of their marketing and advertising efforts, which may or may not be in line with their success in building valuable customer relationships.

Obviously, marketing is a key to success for most organizations. However, a sole focus on marketing will not enable an organization to be successful.

Service Focus

The service focus of many organizations is a legacy from the customer satisfaction emphasis of the early 1980s. The belief here is that if customer service is optimized, customers will continue to frequent your business.

There is no denying that providing good service can lead to customer satisfaction and ongoing loyalty. However, service alone cannot retain customers, much less optimize customer value. If an organization did anything and everything to improve service levels—whether it's reducing check-in lines at a hotel, increasing call center staff at peak periods, or increasing the number of grocery checkouts open during rush hour—would customer value peak? Customers may be more satisfied, but high levels of service have become the norm (i.e., the cost of entry) rather than a critical differentiator.

Customer Focus

Finally, there are those organizations that practice a product, sales, channel, marketing, or service focus but also progress to the customer-focused stage. Maintaining a customer focus is the key to any organization's success in today's marketplace. How can you tell if yours is truly a customer-focused organization?

Broadly speaking, is your organization's primary focus on acquiring, deepening, and retaining customer relationships? Is your business model based on optimizing value delivered to customers to maximize value received from customers? Are your customers at the core of your organization's value system, and the unifying force across business units and functions? To put this into more concrete terms, the checklist in Figure 6-2 provides defining characteristics of customer-focused organizations.

The Leadership Imperative

At this point, it should be clear that implementing customer relationship management is not for the faint of heart. Implementing CRM requires the vision and leadership of senior management for all of the reasons identified in this chapter. CRM may necessitate a sweeping change across your organization. Therefore, your ability to manage change represents a prime determinant of your success.

The importance of an overall CRM vision cannot be overstated. Senior management must define a vision that should drive all of your CRM strategies and tactics. Therefore, this vision needs to be broad enough to garner organizational support and enable very diverse strategies and initiatives. Yet this vision needs to provide cohesive, meaningful direction to those tasked with implementation.

Your organization's core culture may need to change in ways that further customer relationships over individual or departmental interests. This requires strategic positioning with many areas of your organization, some of which will fail to see the benefit. Therefore, this CRM change initiative requires effective, consistent ongoing internal communication. You must share and explain the reasons why your organization is implementing CRM. Since this initiative is going to affect different internal constituencies in very different ways, you should customize your communications to each group. It is critical to have all of your employees "thinking like the customer" (see Figure 6-3).

Whether CRM appears to be an obvious necessity or a sizable new opportunity for your organization, you need to be able to communicate this vision and then provide the leadership and direction in order to deliver on this promise.

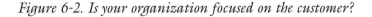

Figure 6-2. Is your organization focused on the customer?

✔ Do you have a clearly defined mission and business strategy, driven by customer needs and the performance of customer relationships?

✔ Do you have strategic planning processes to identify customer and market opportunities?

✔ Have you established clear CRM goals and objectives, specific to functions and departments, and related to customer acquisition, development, retention, and reactivation?

✔ Are your CRM mission and vision, goals, and objectives shared across and well understood throughout your organization?

✔ Does your organization vigorously channel time and resources towards customer needs, providing value to the customer, obtaining loyalty, and managing customer relationships?

✔ Does your organization understand your customers? Is there a common definition and understanding of who your customers really are?

✔ Do your customers inherently recognize the value that your organization places on their business and their ongoing relationships?

✔ Are your investments in customer relationships based on the potential value of each customer to your organization?

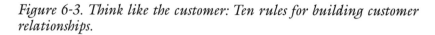

Figure 6-3. Think like the customer: Ten rules for building customer relationships.

1. The "average customer" does not exist—get to know us.

2. Make our experience special: Give us something to talk about.

3. If something is wrong, fix it quickly.

4. Guarantee our satisfaction.

5. Trust us, and we'll trust you.

6. Don't take us for granted.

7. Our time is as important as your time.

8. The details are important to us—they should be to you, too.

9. Employ people who are ready, willing, and able to serve us.

10. We care whether you're a responsible corporate citizen.

Focus: Defining and Designing CRM with Your Customers

Derrith Lambka, Founder, Insights for Action
(www.InsightsForAction.com)

In the "old days," products were designed by engineers for engineers—not for the intended customer who would be using the product.

That changed. Companies started empowering product marketing departments to understand customer needs, prioritize those needs based on what was most important to customers, and define product features for the research and development (R&D) teams. These marketing teams conducted extensive research to understand the customer's world and priorities, which then guided them in defining new products and enhancements. They shifted focus from "This is what we like" to "This is what our customers like."

Marketing teams also kept customers involved throughout the process. They conducted usability research on prototypes of the product to make certain determinations: Could the customers figure out how to use the product? What did they think about the feature set? After the product was in use, more research was conducted to learn what customers liked and didn't like. These insights were used to help product marketing in defining future products or product enhancements. This process has become standard now in product development.

In my experience, most companies do not apply these same customer-involved principles when defining customer programs or customer interactions. Instead, committees decide. Well-meaning web technologists decide. The customer is absent or abstract during the definition process. Or worse, once the site or customer loyalty program is up and running, the company learns customers don't like it. The company faces a costly and time-consuming redesign.

Yet companies seem surprised, nonetheless, that:

- So many customers are abandoning their online shopping carts.
- So few customers are shifting from "calling to clicking" when they need technical support assistance.
- Only 5–10 percent of customers open the "helpful" CRM e-mail messages that the company sends out. That means 90–95 percent of customers receiving these messages don't even consider them valuable enough to open, much less read or act on.
- Customer loyalty is so low, and there are so few advocates—customers who proactively tell their friends how great a product or service is.

Most companies do not understand their customers' total experience—that is, all the interactions a customer has, or wants to have, at each stage of the product lifecycle. And they do not seem to develop strategies to deal with the so-called "off ramps"—those interactions that cause the customer to choose not to buy, to delay a purchase, to choose another brand, or to return a product.

Fewer companies still look at the total customer experience—all the ways the customer interacts with the company—to learn what is most important to customers and to learn what works and what doesn't work. In short, they do not typically understand their customers' priorities.

Without understanding their customers' priorities, companies may focus on a program or website feature that a customer considers a "nice to have," not a "must have." They lose business because they have been focused on areas that are not most critical to their customers. Beware: What may be cool to a web developer may not be cool to a customer.

Most companies talk about being customer-focused. But most company actions tell otherwise. Most companies are completely unaware of how their customers and prospective customers interact with the various areas of the company or how customers use their products/services. Sure, the people answering the company's phones, the webmasters who get all those e-mail complaints, and the salespeople at customer sites know what the customer experience is like and what most frustrates customers. But these customer-facing employees seem to have little clout to change the process or product. They are there to react to problems, not to try to prevent them in the first place. They're the business world's version of a Band-Aid.

So how can your company walk the talk of being customer-focused? Here is a recommended course of action:

1. Involve your customers in defining programs and their ideal experience.
2. Understand your customers' definition of a job well done. You want to understand what they consider unacceptable, a must-do, a nice-to-do, and what would actually "wow" them. You want to do this before you roll out a CRM program or an e-commerce site.
3. Keep the customer involved throughout the "define and design" stage. This will help you hone the program and work out the kinks in a preventive way before the program or service is introduced.
4. Remember that customers at different stages of their "relationship" with you should be treated differently. Communication with your customers is like dating: They find you or you find them. The first interaction you have with them—e-mail,

in person, on the web, or over the phone—is pivotal.

5. Learn from others. Great information on best practices for e-mail marketing, customer loyalty, website
development, and CRM is readily available from books, magazines, conferences, and on the Web.

6. Focus on continuous improvement. Track what is working and what isn't with your customers. Understand their priorities and identify three things you can do that would most dramatically improve your customers' satisfaction, repurchase habits, and loyalty (and your bottom line). Make incremental and regular changes. Show customers you are listening and learning from them.

CHAPTER SEVEN

ORGANIZING AROUND CRM

Business focus, commitment, and understanding of the required change processes are essential components of the CRM transformation. However, even the most committed organizations will find it very challenging to make the necessary transformation if they do not address critical internal issues.

There are essentially three issues that a company must address in order to organize around customers. They are:

1. The organizational structure that will most effectively optimize customer relationships
2. The related owners of CRM initiatives in the organization
3. Employee training, performance measurement, and compensation

All three of these issues deserve explanation in the context of an overarching CRM transformation.

Defining the Organizational Structure

CRM is an enterprisewide initiative. It requires that all areas of the organization work toward the common goal of building stronger customer relationships. Anything less can mean the difference between success and failure. If we look at the organizational structure dimension of the CRM transformation map (see Figure 7-1), we see that prior to the optimal customer management, most organizational structures focus on some combination of product, place, promotion, channels, and contacts.

Product Management

In many companies, product managers function as key decision makers, developing, managing, pricing, promoting, and distributing products for their product line. Product managers operate independently, each looking at the same universe of customers and prospects, trying to find those who are most likely to buy.

For example, in financial services, there are product managers responsible for deposit, consumer loan, mortgage loan, and credit card products. Each of these product managers is independently mining the customer base, attempting to sell products from their specific line. The result is all too often disjointed, redundant, or conflicting communications to the customer.

Place Management

In addition to product managers, many companies emphasize place management with a multitiered organizational structure. Store or branch managers report to regional managers who in turn report to divisional vice presidents. These divisions are often organized along geographic lines. Managers' incentives are based on the performance of their store or branch. That incentive is typically related to acquisition and total sales, but not to retention of

Figure 7-1. Organizational structure transformation.

ORGANIZATIONAL STRUCTURE					
Product Management	Place Management	Promotion Management	Channel Management	Contact Management	Customer Management

©1999 Nykamp Consulting Group.

customers. Competition among stores or branches, regions, and divisions is encouraged, with special recognition going to those who maximize sales. From a customer standpoint, the result is a company with many different faces and no cohesive strategy.

Promotion Management

In most organizations, marketing and advertising managers focus on specific marketing promotions and efforts. Some or all of their tasks may be outsourced to agencies or other third parties. Staff is typically organized around the tactical requirements of placing ads, coordinating with agencies, and producing and distributing other marketing materials.

With the advent of more sophisticated marketing systems, marketers have greatly improved their ability to track and measure marketing effectiveness. They are now able to report results of each campaign, quantifying response and conversion rates, cost per acquisition, and incremental lift (i.e., any net profit generated above and beyond a predefined amount). However, few attempts have been made to measure or manage promotion effectiveness from a customer perspective. How many times have different customer groups been contacted by your organization? What series of contacts has led to optimal customer value? What series of contacts has actually decreased customer value? What is the point of diminishing returns—that is, at what point should we stop trying to communicate with a customer?

In most organizations, the focus is on the performance of each campaign or marketing program, without any longitudinal view of the effectiveness of contact streams over time.

Channel Management

During the 1980s and 1990s, most organizations expanded sales through multiple channels. Retailers added catalogs, and catalogers added retail outlets. Financial services institutions added automated voice response (AVR) telephone service and online banking. Cable added the ability to purchase pay-per-view movies by telephone or through "impulse" remote control. Today, companies relate with customers on the sales floor, at customer service counters, over the telephone through voice recognition unit (VRU) capabilities or "live" customer service departments, through e-mail and online stores, and through catalogs and direct mail.

The organizational structure has oftentimes expanded by adding management counterparts and staff responsible for each new channel. This continued expansion of channels and customer touchpoints has led to competition and contradictions among channel organizations, with each vying for the primary role. For example, retail stores and management are often at odds with their direct marketing and/or e-commerce counterparts. E-commerce teams are often snubbing their traditional sales and marketing channels, which still may account for 99 percent of sales. These organizational divisions can prove to be counterproductive, rather than supportive of each other, realizing the synergies possible within a multichannel environment.

Contact Management

In contact management, the organization begins to realize the nature and number of interactions with customers. The focus at this stage is on using historical data to increase the relevance of each contact. A sales representative, for example, will track the issues that were discussed with the customer during the last call and use that information to converse more appropriately during the next call.

Contact management is focused primarily on outbound sales and marketing contacts and the relevance of those contacts. From an organizational standpoint, dedicated sales and service representatives are assigned to specific customers and customer segments. Organizations in this stage are often focused on customer satisfaction and service quality. Contact management can prove to be a successful means of understanding customer interactions. However, this tactical approach seldom addresses the broader customer investment and management strategies that need to be in place across your organization.

Customer Management

Organizations are now starting to realize that they literally have to organize around their customers, making segment managers an integral part of the organizational structure. The role of segment managers is to optimize the profitability and loyalty of their customer portfolio. This may be a tightly defined, small pool of key accounts. Alternatively, it may be a very large group of a million one-time customers or expired accounts. The importance of practical, well-defined customer segmentation cannot be overstated.

Ultimately, segment managers are responsible for acquisition, development, and retention of their customer segment. Organizationally, segment managers:

- Collaborate with product managers to customize products to the needs of their customers.
- Work with marketing groups to develop communications that are most relevant to customers.
- Evaluate promotion and response history in order to identify optimum promotion frequencies and then design dynamic customer- or segment-specific contact strategies.
- Work with channel and customer service managers to differentiate sales and service options based on customer value and preferences at each point of contact.

Segment managers need to serve as customer representatives, or ambassadors, in providing the most appropriate mix of products and services to their customers.

The Drivers of CRM Initiatives

One of the more difficult challenges an organization will face in the transformation process relates to the ownership of CRM initiatives. Does CRM belong in the marketing department? The e-business area? The database marketing department? The information systems area? The customer service group? The sales channel? It seems that all of these areas are laying stake to the claim. Logical arguments could be made in favor of each of these areas.

Customer relationship management efforts require a primary initial owner. CRM is difficult to implement and requires strong leadership and ongoing commitment. Yet none of these functional areas is optimal, and all could lead to less than successful results. CRM therefore requires a department of its own.

The New Customer Relationship Department

The proposed solution involves establishing a stand-alone Customer Relationship Department that is responsible for optimizing customer relationships at all points of interaction. It is a job that no other single department could effectively handle.

What will a Customer Relationship Department actually do? This group will ensure that CRM strategies are successfully implemented across the organization. The Customer Relationship Department will be responsible for:

- Investment decisions relative to CRM programs and processes. This is an ongoing responsibility, as CRM capabilities will evolve and new CRM opportunities will continue to present themselves to your organization.
- Definition of unique customer segments and identification of their needs, attitudes, product affinities, and loyalty drivers. Segment managers need to reside within the Customer Relationship Department to serve as experts on specific customer groups.
- Related education of the organization on the unique needs of customer segments.
- Definition of the optimal contact strategy for each customer segment and subsegment based on that customer group's unique behavior, channel preferences, and long-term potential.
- Management, or at least coordination, of all interactions of various functional groups (e.g., sales, service, and marketing) with customers.
- Identification of the tools and technologies that will enable an organization to optimize customer interactions.

These responsibilities may currently be allocated to staff in sales, marketing, service, and/or information systems. However, these customer relationship responsibilities need to be formalized in one department so that they will be adopted across the organization. Companies such as Microsoft, American Express, Bell South, and Hewlett-Packard have discovered that centralized customer-centric groups within the organization can ensure a more cohesive customer experience.

The Customer Relationship Department should be a cross-functional group, drawing staff from all customer-contact groups within the company. Department members should have skill sets in:

- Change management
- Customer valuation
- Customer interaction and integrated communications
- Customer information management
- Training and performance measurement

If you put this all together, doesn't the Customer Relationship Department balloon in size? It could, but the solution is to identify those individuals who can lead the charge and serve as liaisons to implementation teams in the existing departments. It is a consultative role; when possible, the implementation should take place within the existing functional groups.

Staff Training, Performance Measurement, and Compensation

We have addressed the concept of a Customer Relationship Department and the related organizational structure that may be necessary to support CRM. A third and equally important component relates to the staff training, performance measurement, and compensation practices of your organization.

Staff Training

Staff training is crucial to the success of any CRM initiative. Announcing a new focus on the customer will not be sufficient to change the behavior of most employees. The organization will require ongoing training initiatives focused on:

- *CRM Vision, Strategies, and Goals.* One of the important elements of the leadership action plan mentioned in Chapter 5 is ongoing communication of the CRM vision for the organization. Ideally, senior management should hold regular sessions with all employees to review the corporate CRM vision and discuss the strategies that are currently being implemented. Executives can help to ensure success by communicating their enthusiasm, commitment, and customer focus during each of these meetings.

- *Individual and Group Roles and Responsibilities for CRM.* As the organizational structure changes, employees will require training to address changes in their roles and responsibilities. Training is a critical success factor for change management. Training sessions should address the processes and procedures that have changed, why and how the new processes are expected to affect employees, and, ultimately, their interactions and relationships with customers.

- *Adoption of New Systems.* Employees will also require additional training on new CRM systems or modifications to existing systems. Employees need training on the systems they use to collect, maintain, and access customer information. In addition to any necessary functional training, employees should be provided with the understanding of how their jobs fit into the broader scope of CRM within the organization.

- *Customer Needs.* Most employees are brought into the organization and/or trained for specific functional tasks, from accounting to inventory management, from product development to sales. These functional tasks are typically well defined and relate to the creation, delivery, and measurement of an organization's product offerings. Therefore, the concept of understanding and meeting customers' needs is often ancillary and not a part of performance measurement efforts. Obviously, the ability to understand and meet customers' needs is key to an organization's future livelihood, and therefore it deserves focus and emphasis within training programs.

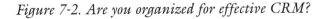

Figure 7-2. Are you organized for effective CRM?

✔ Is senior management tasked with ensuring that the organization understands and is meeting customers' needs? Are they responsible for ensuring that the CRM vision and goals are understood throughout the organization?

✔ Is management accountable for the P&L of customer performance, and responsible for measuring and monitoring customer performance?

✔ Are customer relationship responsibilities clearly defined, assigned, and understood, and are results measured and rewarded?

✔ Are customer-centric performance standards established and monitored at all customer touchpoints?

✔ Does your organization view all customer communications as important, and manage them so they are consistently superior, and relevant to the customer?

✔ Are policies and procedures that are critical to managing customer relationships well documented and consistent across your customer touchpoints?

✔ Are customer-critical functions staffed with well-trained, motivated employees?

✔ Is employee performance measured and rewarded based on meeting customer needs and on successfully serving the customer?

✔ Does your organization have the sales and marketing expertise and resources to succeed in CRM?

✔ Does your organization have the service resources and excellence to succeed in CRM?

✔ Does the organization have the technical expertise and resources to succeed in CRM?

✔ Are there employee training programs designed to develop the skills required for acquiring and deepening customer relationships?

As your CRM efforts continue to advance and as the internal roles and responsibilities of individual employees may change, training becomes even more important because it ensures cohesive, ongoing corporate understanding and capabilities.

Performance Measurement and Compensation

Classic organizational theory has taught us that individuals in a business environment will focus on both what is measured and what is compensated. Modifying the business focus and organization structure and installing new systems will have little or no impact if performance and compensation processes are not addressed.

Traditionally, compensation has been based on some measure of revenues and/or profitability. Performance review and compensation processes should provide incentives for employee behaviors that optimize the value delivered to and received from customers. Acquisition of profitable customers, retention of profitable customers, further penetration of customers through cross-sell efforts, and reactivation of valuable customers through win-back campaigns are all much more meaningful measures of employee performance. The key for many organizations is the ability to consistently measure these activities across the organization.

These three factors—organizational structure; CRM drivers; and employee training, measurement, and compensation—are absolutely critical to the success of your CRM efforts. The checklist in Figure 7-2 provides a series of questions to help you determine whether your organization is organized for effective CRM.

CHAPTER EIGHT

BUSINESS METRICS AND ANALYTICS TO SUPPORT CRM

As you begin the process of changing your business focus from products to customers and prepare to undertake building the organizational structure to support that change in focus, your measures of performance need to change as well. This chapter discusses the business metrics and analytics that support your organization's transformation to CRM.

Understanding customers and developing customer intelligence will obviously drive many of your initial CRM initiatives. New business metrics and supporting analyses are also required in order to continually monitor the customer dimension of your business.

Transforming Business Metrics

It is not accidental that at least some of the early stages of business metrics transformation (see Figure 8-1) resemble those on the business focus and organizational structure dimensions of the

Figure 8-1. Business metrics tramsformation.

BUSINESS METRICS					
Product Performance	Place Performance	Program Performance	Customer Revenues	Customer Satisfaction	Customer Lifetime Value and Loyalty

©1999 Nykamp Consulting Group.

Transformation Map. Traditionally, organizations have developed the metrics necessary to support a particular business focus or measure performance of a specific division. Therefore, it is not surprising that most organizations find that different parts of the organization are focused on very different metrics. Seldom are customer-oriented metrics linked to measures of product or place performance.

As with other dimensions of the CRM Transformation Map (originally introduced in Chapter 4), an organization should not abandon all existing metrics related to the performance of products, stores, and marketing campaigns. Rather, the new customer-focused metrics need to meld with the existing measures in order to ensure that the customer dimension has an integral focus.

Product, Place, and Program Performance Measures

Most organizations today have business performance measures related to these three P's—product, place, and program performance.

Product Performance Metrics and Analyses

When an organization is focused on products, time and resources are spent answering questions such as:

- What were our total private-label product sales over this last quarter?
- Which products are most profitable?
- Can we lower the price on soft lines to increase the sales volume? If so, by how much?

These are essential measures, provided that they aren't the only measures of performance.

Place Performance Metrics and Analyses

When a company is focused on measuring productivity and profitability across branches or store-specific regions or territories, it answers questions such as:

- What are last week's results by store location and type?
- Are the Midwest region's margins consistently higher than the West's margins?
- How do e-commerce sales compare to retail sales?

As with product measures, these measures of performance by place are essential.

Program Performance Metrics and Analyses

For organizations driven by sales and marketing, performance measures relate to:

- How many leads did we generate on the spring discount promotion?
- What was the return on marketing investment from that "best customer" campaign?
- Which customer service script has proven to be most productive?

Most organizations rely on some combination of product, place, and program metrics as their core measures of business success. You will find far fewer who have adopted any customer-related metrics as core business measures of success. While many organizations may generate customer metrics—often within the sales and marketing departments—few of these metrics are considered integral to business operations. Why?

First and foremost, most organizations "grew up" with a focus on products or channels; that is naturally where the measurement also began. Second, many organizations have traditionally lacked a comprehensive view of their customers' behaviors, making customer metrics difficult if not impossible to calculate.

Relatedly, customer metrics by their nature can be more difficult to calculate and may be subject to change, as customers are much more dynamic than products or geographic locations. Nonetheless, as described throughout this book, measuring customer behaviors and dynamics is critical to your continued success.

Customer Revenues

At minimum, every organization—regardless of industry, size, or location—should have a solid understanding of the relative, if not absolute, amount of business that each customer generates. Your organization should understand:

- Who are your top-ten customers in terms of revenue?
- Do 20 percent of your customers generate 80 percent of your revenues?
- Are revenues from any customer segment increasing or declining?

Obviously, these are essential measures to continually monitor and apply to business decisions.

Customer Satisfaction

Customer satisfaction studies are often the focus of primary research efforts. These studies frequently address customer service and support issues and as such may provide answers to the following:

- For which customer segments has satisfaction increased or decreased?
- How have improvements in call center practices increased satisfaction?
- How do highly satisfied customers differ from highly dissatisfied customers?

Unfortunately, customer satisfaction statistics are often limited in their application because they are seldom correlated with customer behaviors. Interestingly, these correlations may not be what you expect. For example, some studies have found that service dissatisfaction has an inverse correlation with attrition; that those customers who expressed some level of dissatisfaction were actually less likely to leave. The finding in this case was that those who were willing to invest time in a satisfaction study were actually those who had loyalty to the brand. It is obviously important to understand how satisfaction data may or may not be related to your customers' behavior.

Customer Loyalty and Value

Understanding customer spending behavior and satisfaction, and the potential relationship between these factors, is obviously also important. The critical results of customer behavior and satisfaction are customer loyalty and value. A solid understanding of loyalty and value and the factors that influence them provides a basis for all of your CRM strategies and programs.

At this stage on the Transformation Map, an organization will have created unique customer segments and developed relationship profitability and lifetime value (LTV) metrics. Questions answered at this stage increase significantly in number and include:

- Who are our unique customer segments?
- Does our organization have profitable relationships with all of our customers?
- How can we increase customer profitability?
- What drives loyalty for our most profitable customers? How do we increase customer loyalty?
- How can we increase the cross-purchase activity of our customers?
- Which prospects should our organization focus on in order to "clone" our best customers?

These people-based metrics will encourage your organization to focus on customers, as well as provide relevant measures of CRM success over time.

How to Develop Customer-Focused Metrics and Analyses

Comprehensive customer intelligence is not developed overnight. Rather, it is an iterative process that includes collecting relevant customer data, building on your customer intelligence incrementally, and communicating results across the organization with a customer scorecard.

Collecting the Right Customer Data

A first step and ongoing process should focus on the collection, cleaning, and consolidation of data on your customers. Figure 8-2 suggests some of the key attributes that you should attempt to gather and maintain on each of your customers.

In terms of where and how you gather the information outlined in Figure 8-2, the answer varies greatly based on your business model. If you sell directly to your customers—with minimal channel intervention—the information that is collected with each transaction (whether through point-of-sale, the sales force, the Web, over the phone, or through the mail) should serve as your primary source. If you are committed to relationships with your customers, it is obviously critical to link transactions to specific individuals. Some channels, media, and related business models are more conducive to this information gathering than others.

If there is a channel partner between you and your end-customers, or if there are other difficulties in gathering individual transaction information, you will need to be much more creative, and more patient. Warranty programs have proved to be one means for manufacturers to gather customer purchase information; value-added web-based services can also encourage your customers to identify themselves to you. Support services, customer hot lines, loyalty cards—all are other ways to continually gather information on who your customers are and what they do.

Increasing Your Customer IQ

You can follow a logical series of analyses to create a solid foundation of customer intelligence and develop processes to grow and expand your customer IQ over time. This analysis relates to:

Figure 8-2. Key customer attributes.

Answer the following questions with your organization's data:

Who are our customers?
- ❏ Unique customer identifier
- ❏ Customer name
- ❏ Name of organization for which the customer works
- ❏ Name of department or group within organization in which the customer works
- ❏ Title, role in organization, or other designation

Where can we reach our customers?
- ❏ Home address
- ❏ Business address
- ❏ Phone number
- ❏ E-mail address
- ❏ Fax number

What are our customers' key characteristics?

Consumer
- ❏ Gender
- ❏ Age
- ❏ Household size
- ❏ Estimated income
- ❏ Presence of children
- ❏ Segment classifications

Business
- ❏ Industry classification
- ❏ Number of employees
- ❏ Annual revenues
- ❏ Number of locations
- ❏ Role of individual in purchase process

How do customers prefer to interact with us?
- ❏ Media preference (e.g., mail, e-mail, phone, fax)
- ❏ Channel preference (e.g., Web, retail store or branch, salesperson, phone)
- ❏ Opt-in or opt-out for any media or specific communications

What has been our history of interactions?
- ❏ Outbound marketing promotion history
- ❏ Outbound sales contact history
- ❏ Inbound customer-initiated queries

What has been our customers' purchase behavior?
- ❏ Purchase dates
- ❏ Number of transactions
- ❏ Items
- ❏ Prices
- ❏ Channels utilized
- ❏ Sale versus nonsale purchases
- ❏ Returns
- ❏ Exchanges

What is the customer's value to our organization?
- ❏ Revenue to date
- ❏ Profitability to date
- ❏ Estimated lifetime value
- ❏ Estimated share of wallet
- ❏ Estimated probability of response to specific promotions
- ❏ Estimated probability of specific purchases
- ❏ Estimated probability of attrition
- ❏ Estimated probability of nonpayment or bad debt

- Customer profiling
- Customer segmentation
- Customer valuation
- Customer lifecycle
- Customer attitudes
- Changes in customers over time

Customer Profiling. Profiling is a core knowledge discovery process that serves as the basis for all subsequent customer-focused analytical efforts. Profiling typically involves summarizing customer characteristics, such as demographics, firmographics (i.e., company demographics), geography, tenure, purchase recency and frequency, channel and media usage, and service usage. Profiling can provide strategic insights into the most fundamental issues of relationship management by giving you an overview of who your customers are.

Customer Segmentation. Customer segmentation is a means of identifying unique customer groups who have different needs, expectations, and purchase behaviors. Each segment can then be described both quantitatively and qualitatively in terms of product usage and other purchase behavior and characteristics. These customer segments form the foundation for defining CRM strategies related to product development, customer service, sales and marketing, retail and field operations, and all customer interactions.

Try to create a "resume" for each segment of customers. What would you say about them? What is most notable? These narrative "resumes" can allow you to deliver relevant, customized marketing messages and appeals. More important, the "credentials" of each segment will enable you to set quantifiable goals in terms of future purchase activity and profitability.

Customer Valuation. Beyond current revenues, there are several measures of value that should be evaluated for your individual customers and summarized by customer segment:

- *Profitability.* This is defined as customer revenues less all costs of providing goods and servicing customers.
- *Lifetime Value (LTV).* LTV forecasts annual profitability over the expected lifetime of a customer, using net present value financial calculations. There are many ways of looking at future value. Very basic LTV calculations assume statistics of spending, with the primary variant being attrition over time. More powerful LTV calculations also include cross-purchase behavior and other changes in spending behavior over time.
- *Share of Wallet.* This specifically is a measure of customer loyalty. The share-of-wallet metric estimates the percentage of business a customer is giving you, versus your competitors. If they are spending $27 a month with your grocery chain, are you assuming they are giving you all of their business or might there be some left on the table?

Each of these value measures provides a different dimension to your understanding of your customer relationships today and what those relationships might become in the future.

Customer Lifecycle. This analysis seeks to uncover stages of a customer's relationship with you, and with your products and services over an extended period of time. The result of this analysis should yield answers to these questions:

- When does a customer initially purchase your products or services? What are their characteristics in this initial stage, and what related needs are they typically looking to initially fulfill?
- What product or services do new customers tend to buy?
- How do changes in customer characteristics then drive their needs, their use of specific channels, and the products and services that they buy?

Think of the relationship between a financial services firm and an emerging business. The relationship will likely begin just days after the business is formed, with the need for a checking account.

As the business grows and employees are hired, both product and service needs expand. Although this lifecycle is less than predictable, there are definitely patterns that should be recognized and acted upon.

Organizations are increasingly using the customer lifecycle to identify ways in which the customer experience can be tailored or customized to add value and therefore increase customer satisfaction and loyalty. This analysis allows the organization to more accurately anticipate customer needs and proactively meet those needs.

Expanding the Picture: Customer Attitudes. CRM also requires a thorough understanding of the values, opinions, and expectations that shape customers' purchase decisions. Although some information can be inferred through purchase activity itself, attitudinal information can best be gathered through primary research. Surveys targeted at representative subsets of customers from each segment will expand your customer IQ.

This research needs to be very targeted; if you had the opportunity to ask your customers only three questions, what would they be? While there is obviously no limit to the amount of information you could try to gather from your customers, you will reach a point of diminishing returns. Therefore, focus on information you would consider "need to know" versus information that's "nice to know." The results of the initial primary research may provide guidance on the information that should be more aggressively captured from individual customers at the point of contact—such as through informal surveys at the time of order entry, on the website, or at the customer service desk.

Remaining Relevant: Tracking Customer Changes. Customers change. Their households expand or contract, their earnings increase or decrease, and their needs, attitudes, and preferences shift overnight or over much longer periods of time. Similarly, your business changes—your markets, products and services, pricing, and standard business practices are intentionally or unintentionally in a state of continual movement, which may have an even greater impact on the change in your customer base. This continual change is something that most of us would prefer to forget. It can wreak havoc on our strategic plans, programs, segments, and profiles. Yet acknowledging and managing this change is the only way that you can remain relevant to your customer base.

Communicating and Applying Customer Intelligence

It is clearly not enough to just collect, create, and maintain customer intelligence. Customers will continue to reveal attitudes and preferences—and give you business—only if you demonstrate that you are tailoring and improving their experience based on the information they provide. Remember, customers have increasingly higher expectations of their service providers. This means that organizations need to apply critical customer information at all customer touchpoints, just as they need to communicate key customer-focused metrics to all employees throughout the organization on a regular basis. One of the most effective means of summarizing customer information across your organization is through the development and distribution of a customer scorecard.

The Customer Scorecard. Figure 8-3 provides an example of a customer scorecard. Think of the scorecard as a meaningful snapshot of your customers. This scorecard should not just be a set of statistics. Rather, it should tell a story, communicate knowledge of customer behavior, and suggest new strategies for a segment of customers or across your base.

The first step in creating a scorecard is determining the customer group or groups that you are going to measure—are you providing a synopsis of your customer base as a whole or of several customer segments? You may want to start simple, with one scorecard on all your customers, then branch into segment-specific measures over time.

The next step involves defining the key customer-based metrics that are most relevant to your organization. Optimally, the annual goal for each metric, for each customer segment, is displayed along with current performance statistics. Some of the metrics you might include in the scorecard are:

Figure 8-3. Customer scorecard.

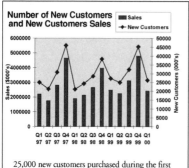

25,000 new customers purchased during the first quarter of 2000, spending more than $2 million. This represents a slight decline in sales dollars relative to the first quarter of 1999. However, the average sales per new customer increased by almost 1% compared with first quarter 1999.

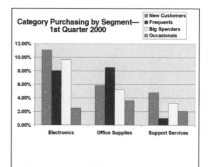

The big spenders and the new customers continue to purchase more often from the Electronics category with no material change from prior months.

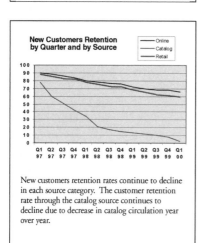

New customers retention rates continue to decline in each source category. The customer retention rate through the catalog source continues to decline due to decrease in catalog circulation year over year.

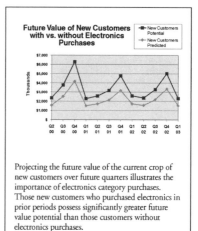

Projecting the future value of the current crop of new customers over future quarters illustrates the importance of electronics category purchases. Those new customers who purchased electronics in prior periods possess significantly greater future value potential than those customers without electronics purchases.

- *Number of Current Customers, by Segment and Tenure.* It is important to understand the number of customers within each segment, and the length of time that they have been your customers. This information will provide insights regarding customer acquisition and retention rates.

- *Product Penetration.* This metric typically identifies the percentage of customers within each segment that have purchased within each major product category. In service industries such as banking or telecommunications, the metric relates to current ownership or usage. In other industries the metric may represent purchase behavior over the past six or twelve months.

- *Cross-Sell.* This measure identifies the number of different products or product categories purchased by customers.

- *Upsell.* You may look for increases in average balance in major product categories or increases in total monthly billings. In retail, the metric may relate to trends in average order size, total market basket (i.e., total sales), or frequency of purchase.

- *Current Profitability.* This is an important metric and can be as simple as reporting margin or as complex as reporting fully loaded customer or household profitability. Some organizations also report important drivers of customer profitability such as total fees or service plan/extended warranty purchases.

- *Lifetime Value or Long-Term Potential.* Changes in average LTV or long-term potential can be attributed to changes in the composition of a customer segment, changes in their behavior, or changes in your products or services.

- *Channel Penetration and Usage.* In many industries, channel usage can have a big impact on customer profitability and lifetime value. For example, airlines are analyzing online versus offline ticket sales. Financial services organizations are analyzing ATM transactions versus the more costly teller transactions. These metrics often address not only the number of transactions but also the associated dollars spent, and perhaps even identify product categories.

- *Customer Service or Satisfaction.* Some organizations also are able to report on the number of customer service support calls in various categories, or trends revealed from ongoing satisfaction surveys.

Figure 8-4. Does your organization have critical CRM metrics?

✔ Do key customer-focused metrics exist, with definitions that are well-understood throughout the organization?

✔ Are customer metrics used to create strategies, make decisions, and act on those decisions?

✔ Are customer metrics shared and rigorously reviewed across the organization on a regular basis?

✔ Are customer perceptions and feedback formally measured and reported across the organization? Is this feedback used to create strategies to positively influence customer perceptions?

✔ Are budgets and investments based on customers' current and potential performance of customer metrics and the customer base?

✔ Are employee performance standards established in areas that impact customer performance? Do performance standards closely relate to improvement of customer metrics?

Keep in mind that the aforementioned metrics represent only some of the metrics that organizations may track. You should carefully define your scorecard metrics to ensure that you are highlighting those that are most important to your organization and industry. Too much information will distort the picture and confuse the story you are trying to tell. Recommended best practices in using CRM metrics are outlined in Figure 8-4.

Remember that your customer scorecard needs to tell a story by highlighting trends over time and providing comparisons by customer segment and other relevant criteria. Scorecard design and ongoing adjustments to reflect changes in your business are critical to your success with this concept.

CHAPTER NINE

TRANSFORMING CUSTOMER INTERACTIONS

Customer interactions are the core of CRM. Every customer relationship is dependent on the quality, consistency, value, and relevance of those interactions. We cannot transform our business focus to customers or optimize customer relationships without transforming the interactions we have with customers at all points of contact.

The Customer Experience Cycle outlined in Chapter 3 is critical to your CRM planning efforts. For many organizations, this process is very revealing because, for the first time, they begin to understand just how many different ways they interact with customers. For example:

- Retailers realize that it is not just the sales clerks on the floor that interact with customers. Other points of contact include:

– The part-time high school student who wraps the baby gift
– The credit department clerk who verifies identification in order to look up a forgotten credit card number
– The direct mail piece promoting the January white sale
– The credit card statement sent by the retailer's credit card partner
– The print advertisement in the Sunday paper
– The cash register receipt from a recent purchase providing a discount coupon for a complimentary product
– The customer service representative at the returns desk who decides whether to give full credit for returned merchandise
– The three-person delivery team who wrestled the new big-screen TV down into the basement

- Banks have fostered an increasingly broad range of interactions with customers as they have tried to move customers to less costly channels. A bank's points of contact today may include:
  – The ATM a customer uses to withdraw cash
  – The inbound automated call center a customer accesses to check a balance or verify a deposit
  – The security guard who directs parking lot traffic into and out of the lot on busy paydays
  – The website a customer accesses to see if the online bill payment was processed
  – The new accounts desk that a customer visits to invest in a certificate of deposit
  – The inbound call center representative a customer reaches when applying for a new "instant approval" auto loan
  – The monthly statement a customer receives at home
  – The TV and radio ads that promote the brand image for the newly merged organization

- The letter customers receive, announcing that their local branch is being closed
- The 1099 tax form a customer receives at year's end

- Even an Internet-based business interacts with customers in many different ways and for many different reasons, such as:
  - When a customer receives a broadcast e-mail announcement of a new merchandise line
  - When a customer initiates an inquiry regarding the status of a recent shipment
  - When a customer calls customer service to find out how to return an item
  - When a customer receives an e-mail, thanking the buyer for a recent purchase with an enclosed coupon for dollars off on the next order
  - When a customer purchases a gift certificate for a friend
  - When a customer browses inventory to locate a desired item
  - When a customer notices the business-banner advertising on another website
  - When a customer flips through the sales flyer enclosed with the merchandise ordered

It is the sum total of these interactions, plus some touchpoints outside the direct control of the organization (see the Focus sidebar "The Elusive Interactions"), that defines the customer's experience with your organization.

Customer Interaction Transformation

Each area of an organization has multiple customer contact points or opportunities for interaction. As the customer interaction dimension of the CRM transformation map (see Figure 9-1) indicates, an organization may be focused primarily on the efficiency of each transaction or, optimally, on customizing the customer experience to provide tangible value.

Focus: The Elusive Interactions

When analyzing customer interactions, it is easy to forget and tempting to exclude those customer touchpoints that are not directly controlled by your organization. As you inventory customer touchpoints, it is important to take a hard look at these more elusive customer interactions that may involve third parties. These interactions often present opportunities for drastic improvement or recalibration to support and enhance the customer experience. Examples include:

- The airport security personnel hired by the airlines to scan luggage. While the airlines view them as third-party service providers, most passengers would view them as part of their experience with the airline.

- The third-party e-commerce affiliate for an Internet portal business. While the two companies view their relationship as a partnership, the customer sees one website and has an overall experience with the site.

- The research company hired by a shopping mall to survey customer preferences. To a customer, an encounter with a researcher is part of the overarching shopping-at-the-mall experience.

- The restaurant, shops, tour and time-share service, and sales personnel, all of whom are located within the lobby of a fine resort. While these individuals all represent separate companies, to a customer they are part of the resort experience.

Figure 9-1. Customer interaction transformation.

CUSTOMER INTERACTION					
Mass Transaction	Opportunistic Promotion	Targeted Campaigns	Segment-Specific Communication	Customer-Contact Integration	Individual Permission-Based Interaction

©1999 Nykamp Consulting Group.

Mass Transaction

In the mass transaction stage, there is a "one size fits all" orientation for marketing, sales, and service contacts. Marketing communications efforts can be characterized as mass advertising and lacking any real customer interaction. Communications and offers are crafted to appeal to the audience at large. Consequently, marketing metrics emphasize frequency and reach of brand image and awareness messages.

As recipients of mass advertising, we recognize the law of averages at play. We may be exposed to several thousand messages a day, only a fraction of which are relevant to our immediate needs and interests. Picture yourself driving along a highway with billboards on your left and right. Your radio pipes in one to two dozen commercials every thirty minutes. You stop for gas, and even the back of your receipt is filled with messages and offers. Ninety-nine percent of these messages may be tuned out; 1 percent may be relevant to the situation at hand.

We have become immune to the clutter and have developed the capability to selectively recognize those messages that matter. A glance at the roadways, the receipts, the banner ads on websites, the blow-in cards in magazines, or TV and radio programming suggests that mass advertising is still alive and strong and designed to appeal to all five senses.

Mass advertising does not continue to survive due to its consumer appeal and relevance; it survives because it is difficult to measure on a return-on-investment basis. It is this very lack of measurement that enables mass advertising to continue—often unchallenged—as a viable communications approach.

Similarly, at this mass transaction stage, both sales and service are primarily focused on coverage. Driven by the efficiency of transactions, there is typically little or no capture of customer information beyond the necessary details of the transaction. Performance metrics relate to cost per sale, the length of lines at checkout stands, or how quickly a customer's transaction can be processed. When asked to collect customer information, there is often resistance from order entry or retail operations due to a belief that it just cannot be done without significantly decreasing efficiency. Surprisingly, this strict focus on efficiency is often unfounded (see Focus sidebar "Do You Want It Quickly or Correctly?").

Focus: Do You Want It Quickly or Correctly?

Sometimes, in an effort to please our customers, we make very flawed assumptions about what may be most important to them. This is particularly true when organizations are looking broadly at the customer's total experience, in which case there are many different opportunities to improve sales, service, and marketing elements of the experience. The following story illustrates this point:

> A certain bank (which we will refer to as ABC Capital) was focused on increasing customer service and satisfaction in the face of new competition. On the basis of the number of customer complaints, the bank felt that its highest CRM priority was to decrease the time customers spent waiting in line in retail branches. These long lines were attributed to a steady increase in the bank's customer base, combined with the antiquated computer systems processing transactions. The bank's anticipated CRM initiatives would entail significant investments in new computer systems to speed up processing, as well as extensive remodeling and expansion of retail branches.

Before moving ahead with these costly but seemingly necessary investments, ABC Capital decided to hire a research firm to analyze customer satisfaction relative to services received. ABC Capital felt that this work would confirm its planned branch initiatives.

The research firm used conjoint analysis to quantify the relative importance of service features offered by ABC and to identify the trade-offs customers were willing to make. This technique was used to analyze the customer experience across all contact touchpoints throughout the organization. The focus, however, was on the retail teller line, since this was the area with the greatest volume of customer contact as well as the greatest potential investments in retooling initiatives.

The analysis was relatively complex and involved extensive survey work by customer segment. Findings revealed that:

- Time spent waiting in line was not the most important service attribute.
- Customers felt that expanded lobby hours and tellers' ability to handle a broader range of transactions were significantly more important (see Figure 9-2).
- These results varied by customer characteristics. Therefore, modifications to services could be made at the branch level, based on the distribution of the customer base.

Needless to say, this investment in understanding customer preferences and priorities spared ABC Capital from investing in expensive service offerings that may have done little to increase customer satisfaction and may have furthered dissatisfaction.

*Figure 9-2. ABC Capital's customer
satisfaction findings.*

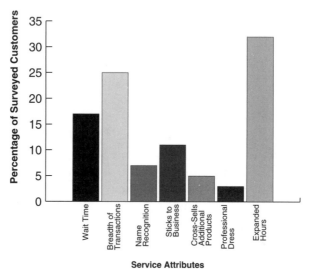

Service Attributes

The simple lesson from this story: While we may know what is important to customers, it is often critical to understand the relative importance of each of the wonderful things you can do to enhance the customer experience. Do you know which ones matter the most to your customers?

Opportunistic Promotion

At the opportunistic promotion stage of customer interaction, marketing and sales use short-term incentives to encourage purchase of a product/service through a combination of mass advertising and broadly distributed direct marketing. Characterized by "product du jour" offers with very little differentiation, sales promotion is a means of creating incentives for immediate purchase. These promotions may be run in a vacuum, with different areas of the organization unknowingly sending conflicting messages to the same customers. Different areas of the organization may even compete for customer spending behavior.

Service personnel in an opportunistic promotion environment are trained to cross-sell specific products based on a customer's current purchase. However, they often lack information about a customer's past purchase behavior, much less on how often a customer may have received an offer in the past.

From a customer standpoint, this lack of coordination often breeds confusion and may erode brand perceptions. You may receive multiple different credit card offers within a week from the same issuer. Each of these efforts may state that "Because you are so special . . . this is the card for you." Could that really be the case?

Targeted Campaigns

In a targeted campaign environment, the organization begins to focus on communicating more efficiently and effectively with customers and prospective customers. Some combination of demographic characteristics, purchase behavior, media consumption, channel usage, and promotion responsiveness is used to develop a targeting strategy. Data mining techniques identify those customers most likely to respond to the offer. However, the promoted products or the specific offer may still be driven from a product or merchandising orientation. The emphasis is on identifying which customers will respond to a given offer, rather than on what customers might need.

In this marketing-centric environment, there are often challenges working with other areas of the organization—ranging from customer care to fulfillment—that may not have been involved in the planning and therefore cannot support the intended implementation.

Segment-Specific Communications

Beyond the coordination of mass and targeted media, many organizations have begun to develop efforts focused on specific customer segments. Segment-specific communications represents the beginnings of a shift in focus to people—that is, the customers—more than the organization's products, programs, and promotions. It involves the ongoing development, refinement, and management of marketing efforts to specific customer segments. Focusing on customer segments allows an organization to tailor communication streams to the needs and interest of each group of customers, and the ability to manage differential investments based on each segment's potential value to the organization.

At this stage, the organization must have consolidated customer data, including customer profiles and behaviors, and a common definition of customer segments across the organization. Ideally, measures of current and potential value for each segment define the allocation of marketing, sales, and service resources.

Segment managers serve as representatives for their respective groups of customers, directing the entire contact strategy for their customer segment. In that role, they also educate the rest of the organization about unique customer attitudes, needs, and preferences related to products, channels, and media.

In addition to the information on and understanding of each customer segment, an organization needs the ability to measure—on both a micro and macro basis—the results of its investments in each segment. This information enables increased customization, interaction, and delivery to each customer segment.

Customer Contact Integration

At the contact integration stage, organizations begin to understand the cumulative impact of all marketing, sales, and service communications on customer performance. Segment managers work with sales and service executives to define the optimal strategies for each customer segment.

Customer information at each point of contact is key. Segment assignment and information about customer behavior and profitability should be available at most, if not all, points of contact. The focus clearly shifts from the efficiency of the interaction to its effectiveness.

At this stage, a customer scorecard becomes an important business metric that links all of the organization's contacts to customer performance. The scorecard (as discussed in Chapter 8) details customer segment performance, measuring improvements related to market penetration, customer profitability, upsell and cross-sell, product penetration, and retention.

The CRM Goal: Individual Permission-Based Interaction

The final stage of customer interaction transformation—individual permission-based interaction—involves two-way customer interactions with increased relevance and specificity. Organizations at this stage are focused on relevance, value, and permission. Interactions are based on an understanding of the specific needs, interests, and behaviors of each customer. Increasingly, interactions are customer-initiated, which inherently means that the timing, media, and channel are specific to customer preferences. Anticipating what customers will need becomes the basis for ongoing, two-way communications. In addition, interactions are permission-based, which means customers may opt-in and opt-out of specific interactions. Customers may specify when, where, why, and how they receive communications from your business.

In the world of one-to-one marketing via the Web, permission marketing in its purest form means "no spam." It's about asking for permission before sending e-mail offers to customers and giving them easy ways to say no thank-you (i.e., opt-out). Most companies are doing an excellent job of gaining permission from customers online, but this approach seems to stop with the online relationship, even though permission is just as important and just as powerful across all aspects of the customer relationship.

In fact, permission should be initiated during the courtship stage, before a prospect even becomes a customer. In the product-push, acquisition-focused world, it's hard to imagine a telemarketer asking a prospect or new customer, "Is this a good time to talk?" or "Is it okay if we call you again when we have other products or new services you might be interested in?" or "What's the best time of day for us to call?" or "Would you prefer to hear from us via telephone, mail, e-mail, or in person?" Yet ideally, if you truly want to have a relationship with customers, that is exactly what you should do. At the very first contact, you should be asking customers what channels they would prefer for future interactions. You should gain permission and then follow through to communicate and interact how and when customers want to hear from you. Asking permission is scary for most marketers, because in their hearts they believe most prospects and customers, if given the choice, would answer, "Don't contact me at all!" But, without

Figure 9-3. Is your organization supporting individual permission-based interactions?

> ✔ Is your brand positioning consistent across all marketing, sales, and service channels?
>
> ✔ Do you understand individual customers' characteristics, needs, preferences, and behaviors?
>
> ✔ Do you have the ability to customize customer interactions to optimize value and loyalty?
>
> ✔ Do you have a process in place to obtain and validate customers' permission to interact with them through a variety of channels? Do you share this information across all customer contact systems and departments?
>
> ✔ Is individual customer information available at every point of contact?
>
> ✔ Do the marketing, sales, and service areas of your organization cooperatively determine integrated customer contact strategies that vary by individual?

permission, either tacit or implied, it really is difficult to have a relationship with customers. The challenge, then, is finding the best ways to secure permission. Relevancy and value can make the difference.

Forming relationships with customers requires that you find relevant common interests. Most organizations understand that a critical component of CRM is dialogue, but they often forget that a meaningful dialogue requires relevancy. Very simply, that means you need to spend time and effort early on understanding who your customers are and what they like and don't like. And you have to remember that customers' likes and dislikes change; over time you also need to track and remember those changes. You need systems and databases that can capture the nuances of the dialogue (e.g., demographics, interests, preferences, and behavior) at each point of contact. Then you need to use that information to ensure relevance in all aspects of the relationship through all channels.

Savvy e-marketers have learned that the key to gaining permission is in providing tangible value. Customers are willing to receive e-mail if they think they will get something of value along the way. That same principle applies to CRM. Customers will seldom prolong a relationship with a company that does not provide them with value. Value can take many forms beyond the immediate value of purchased products or services. Convenience, speed, ease of access, responsiveness, trust, integrity, education, and service excellence are all part, in varying degrees, of the value equation for most customers. This is where relevance and value have to merge. Understanding what constitutes value to a customer will be critical to maintaining and growing the value of the relationship to the organization.

Individual permission-based interaction is a worthy aspiration. Wouldn't you, as a customer, become increasingly loyal to any organization that was truly devoted to this level of interaction? The checklist in Figure 9-3 will help you assess whether your organization supports a two-way customer interaction strategy that is individual- and permission-based.

Optimizing customer interactions is dependent on other internal factors—the business focus, the organizational structure, the business metrics, and the technology that your organization uses—discussed in other chapters of this book. However, as this chapter has illustrated, your customer interaction strategy can in and of itself be the determinant of your success.

Focus: Enabling the Integration of CRM Touchpoints at HP

One of the fundamental requirements of CRM is being able to identify customers uniquely across multiple touchpoints, recognize them as known customers, and have the sum of the knowledge of them available to potentially support any one interaction.

Hewlett-Packard is working to bring this about by implementing a customer identification infrastructure that enables touchpoint integration. Each customer is assigned a unique identifier, as are companies in the business-to-business (B2B) space, stored in a central reference database that is available to all customer-facing applications and programs. This unique key is enabling call center, web, outbound marketing, and sales force data to be easily aggregated in customer data warehouses, and it is providing visibility to all the points at which the customer is touching HP.

"It's very much in tune with our e-services vision—that customer identification is available as a service on the network in real time to any application, database, or person who needs that information," according to Roger Williams, the HP manager responsible for implementing the service.

ility for developers to build and for clients to buy
ology.

ology. Technology continues to quickly progress—rang-
rom data mining and data visualization tools to the abil-
customize websites and drive personalized messaging—
ing an increasingly broad range of CRM applications.

ese and other reasons that this chapter can only be con-
entry in a time capsule. It is written to offer you a frame
ce as to the key systems and technology issues that are
CRM strategy.

mer-Centric Technology Transformation

of systems that process and maintain customer informa-
anged dramatically over the last several years. As shown
nology dimension of the CRM transformation map (see
-1), this shift in technology focus has progressed as

saction processing and data maintenance are the very
functions of any system. While essential, these
ions alone provide little value in a CRM environment.
warehousing, data marts, and increasingly
isticated, customized levels and means of data access
supported the last two decades of sales, service,
eting, and other business applications.
systems world is increasingly focused on having the
t" information at each customer touchpoint, in order
timize the customer's interaction with your
ization. This is easier said than done, since such
ns require significant business planning as well as
ology deployment.

1. Customer-centric technology transformation.

O L O G Y				
Data Maintenance	Data Access	Data Maintenance	Data Marts	Customer Touchpoint Systems

flex
tech

- *Tec
  ing
  ity
  ena

It is for t
sidered a
of refere
linked to

The Cus

The focu
tion has
in the te
Figure 1
follows:

- Tra
  basi
  fun
- Dat
  sop
  hav
  ma
- The
  "rig
  to
  org
  syst
  tech

Figure 1

T E C H

Transaction
Processing

C H A P T E R

SYSTEMS AND TECH SUPPORT CRM

Time in a Bottle

Before we begin to address the curre
port customer relationship managem
that this chapter is, by its very nature,
years, and even in the last few weeks
aspects of CRM reflect extreme innov
exciting, continually changing time to
The major drivers of this change inclu

- *The CRM Movement Itself.* The
  ment has led to an increased in
  tems by an increasingly broad ar
- *Open Systems, and the Related En*
  Just five years ago, the vast
  systems were proprietary ma
  applications. The advent of open

What Is a CRM System?

Systems to support CRM represent an increasingly wide array of operational and analytical, online and offline offerings. For purposes of this chapter, we have divided these systems into the following categories:

- Customer databases
- Marketing applications
- Data mining applications
- Sales force automation (SFA) systems
- Customer care applications
- Online applications

The schematic in Figure 10-2 indicates how an organization may integrate these applications into a business solution. Appendix A provides a complete overview of each of these categories of systems. It is important to note that in today's systems environment:

1. Most organizations have integrated very few of their CRM systems. Sales, service, marketing, and online e-business systems are all stand-alone applications.
2. This integration of many different software applications is the best that one can hope for. There is no single application that supports all CRM needs.

Thus the ongoing change within the CRM systems world.

Back to definitions for a moment. We define a CRM system quite basically as:

Any application that supports the collection, cleansing, and maintenance of, and/or access to, customer information, and that provides this information to appropriate entities in support of CRM applications.

This is an intentionally broad definition that encompasses literally hundreds of applications. The categorization previously listed is

Figure 10-2. Integrated CRM business solution.

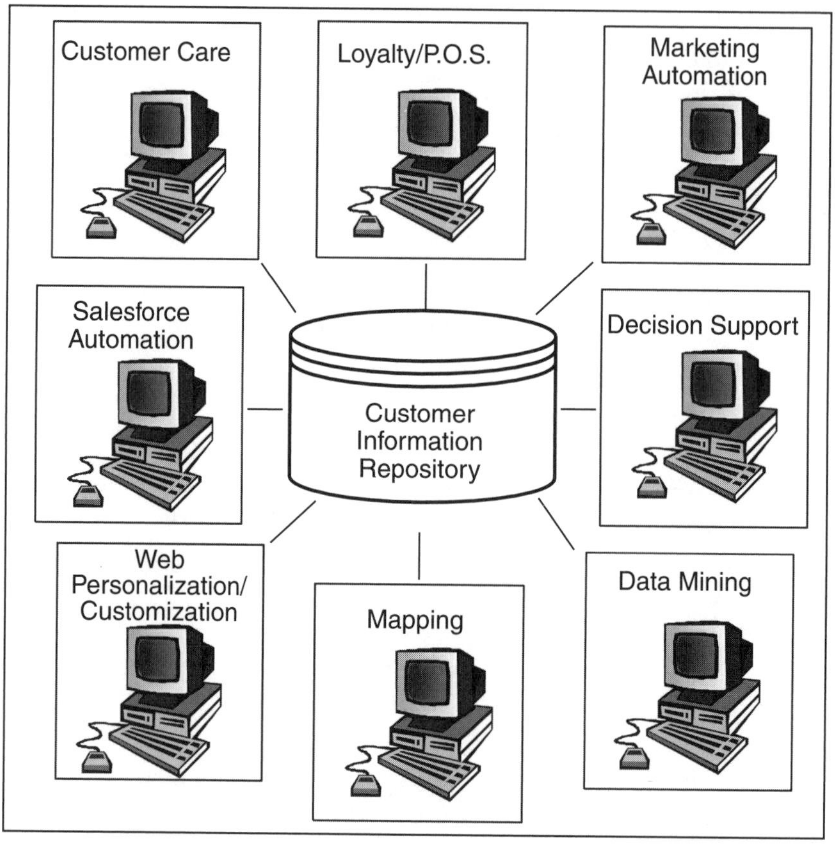

just the beginning of a much more complex CRM systems taxonomy that is beyond the context of this book. What is important to note is that this broad range of functionality, when combined, enhances customer relationships.

The Ultimate CRM Solution

Optimally, there would be one ultimate CRM solution that supports all of your CRM needs. This ultimate CRM solution would support:

- Data collection
- Data cleansing, consolidation, and transformation

- Data maintenance
- Data access to a wide range of users and applications

The ultimate CRM solution would be one single application that could simply be installed and maintained for this variety of needs—one single application that replaces a handful of disparate systems. So why isn't the ultimate CRM solution available today? Why so many niche players? There are a few primary and a broader list of secondary reasons for the current divergence. Primary reasons include:

1. *Operational versus Analytical Systems.* Some of your CRM business needs require very task-based, real-time capabilities. Think of a call center or customer care environment, where a service representative needs to quickly locate a customer record and then capture or provide additional information. Think of your website, where a customer's pattern of behavior or information provided demands an immediate message or customization of the site. These operational systems— often referred to as online transaction processing (OLTP) systems—require relatively lean customer files within reach, for real-time or near-real-time actions and reactions. Compare this to an analytical system, such as a reporting tool that is accessing information in your customer database. Your business needs for trend analysis or other business findings are less than real-time. While you would like to have your questions answered quickly, it is more important to spend a little more time panning through a depth of data to draw the most meaningful conclusions. Call this the "offline" world, where insights rule over instantaneous response.

   One of the reasons that all of our CRM applications do not exist in a single application is that these online and offline systems have traditionally been very different by design. An operational system is built for speed—for processing a transaction and moving on. An analytical system is built for lingering—for in-depth insights.

2. *New CRM Business Applications.* Dozens of e-business and e-marketing applications have emerged almost overnight as independent "e-only" applications. It is obviously much easier for a software company to launch a single-channel, limited-focus application than an enterprise-based CRM system. Yet the advent of e-business begs for the integration of the depth of data in a customer warehouse, with the immediacy of near-real-time reaction.

3. *Organizational Divisions of Responsibility.* The sales, customer service, and marketing groups are usually three independent fiefdoms within an organization. Vendors likewise choose their customers by developing systems to meet the needs of one of these groups rather than dealing with the territorial issues that might arise in trying to work across the organization.

For these and other reasons, these divergent systems coexist in today's systems environment. It is my hope that by the time you are reading this information, the "ultimate CRM solution" is commonplace in the marketplace. Currently, CRM systems vendors from all sides are rushing to bring together an increasingly wide range of functionality in one solution or suite of solutions.

Overarching CRM Systems Issues

Whether you are starting with an offline customer database, or an online customer care application, there are a number of CRM systems issues that should be addressed. These issues can make the difference between your success or failure in being able to support the CRM business applications at hand. The issues discussed here are:

- The value of a customer information management plan
- The essentials of a business case
- Insourcing versus outsourcing
- Data quality
- Data accessibility
- User acceptance

Developing a Customer Information Management Plan

You need to be able to paint the broad picture of how multiple CRM systems and their customer information relate to one another. A customer information management plan should enable you to optimize the value of your customer data assets by painting this picture. A customer information management plan typically addresses:

- Where and how to efficiently collect customer data. There are typically a wide variety of data collection options and current practices varying greatly in efficiency and effectiveness.
- How to transform data into meaningful, practical information. This data may need to be consolidated to an account or household basis, into monthly transaction summaries, or linked to regional sales territories.
- How to readily distribute customer information throughout your organization. Data distribution could encompass a point-of-sale (POS) application or information in sales/ service centers or a decision support system.

Developing a customer information management plan also represents a big opportunity to realize cost efficiencies and increase effectiveness in managing customer relationships across your organization. Shared data cleansing, consolidation, maintenance, reporting, or access tools across systems could provide significant cost reductions and efficiencies.

The development and implementation of this plan, however, can prove to be very challenging. You will likely face the following obstacles:

- *Departmental/Divisional Boundaries.* Various groups within your organization may have differing opinions on data ownership and customer data value. These groups might also have different business goals that may support customer data collection and maintenance efforts, or may defeat these efforts.

- *Deeply Entrenched Systems and Processes.* There may be existing technologies or existing business processes and practices that may be difficult to change.
- *Time and Money.* An enterprisewide initiative such as this could be unsustainably large.

A Recommended Approach. The following steps have proved to be an effective approach for developing a manageable, agreeable plan:

1. *Define where customer data is currently needed or could be utilized across your organization, and why.* You might be surprised in the numbers and variety of data needs; therefore, it is important to differentiate must-haves from nice-to-haves and prioritize.
2. *Conduct a customer information audit.* This effort defines:
   – Where data is currently gathered and how
   – The quantity and quality of this data
   – Where data is maintained and how frequently it is updated
   – How this data is maintained and by whom
   This documentation is crucial because it ensures that all existing data resources are identified.
3. *Based on findings in steps 1 and 2, develop a specification document.* These specifications need to detail data, process, functionality, and architecture requirements. At this stage, avoid identifying specific solutions; rather, focus on detailed business processes and support elements.
4. *Conduct a gap analysis.* This analysis is important for identifying discontinuity between what you have and what you need.
5. *Define a solution that reflects your current situation and your prioritized requirements.* This solution should also take into account "softer" organizational and situational issues, such as the interest levels and capabilities of various departments that could benefit from customer information. Potential solutions may include:

- Design and development of customer data collection and distribution processes and/or mechanisms
- Creation of data collection standards
- Development or improvement of data processing capabilities
- Creation of a conceptual model for an enterprisewide customer information system
- Implementation of a customer-centric data warehouse
- Realignment of internal data sharing practices
- Development of tools providing your organization with common access to customer data
- Alignment of customer information needs with internal data warehouse plans

Developing the plan, while only the beginning, will ensure that any subsequent implementation efforts are in harmony with the broader CRM strategy.

Building a Business Case

The approval process for CRM infrastructure and investments in general has become increasingly complex, as a variety of divisions and subgroups are trying to gain approval for an increasingly broad spectrum of potential solutions. Yet a solid business case is often essential if you are hoping to have your system approved.

The following are a few suggestions to move you successfully beyond that approval meeting with senior management:

1. *Qualify your effort.* Before you approach senior management with your projections, make sure that you actually need and can benefit from a new CRM investment. Do your business economics, CRM capabilities, and organizational characteristics support it? If not, are you able to change or remove any or all of the roadblocks? What are the critical ingredients for success? How many factors do you have working in your favor versus those work-

ing against you? It is okay to fight an uphill battle as long as you first understand the size and scope of the climb and some of the obstacles along the way.

2. *Identify other necessary components, and build a business case for them as well.*

If, for example, you need an increase in budget or a tracking capability to effectively use your CRM system, create separate business cases for these components. Do not include them in the case for the CRM system, but do make it known that there are other pieces of the puzzle that also need to be in place. If you wait until your CRM system is approved to make mention of the other needs, the entire effort may be called into question. If these other elements are not fully approved, your new CRM system will be forced to stand by itself—and it could then live a very short life.

3. *Project results and improvements in a context that reflects your business setting.* You can make the projections—as long as you remain within the bounds of your current environment. Rather than estimating results based on a bigger budget, more resources, or other internal improvements, assume instead that the rest of your world will remain the same.

4. *Gather case studies and success stories, particularly from your own industry and on companies that operate with similar business models.* Do not collect case studies that are not related to your situation, because these often do more harm than good. If your company is not committed to a direct marketing/direct sales model, do not tout L. L. Bean's success as a cataloger. Rather, look for other examples of how companies are gaining benefit from a CRM system while retaining their existing channels.

5. *Prototype.* If a customer database and/or CRM application are new concepts for your organization, you may choose to, or be forced to, prototype. This is not necessarily a bad thing, because a prototyping effort can often strengthen your longer-term solution. If in the short term you can come up with an inexpensive way to maintain a subset of your data or address one of your secondary needs, your focus can then shift to proving the value of the new CRM strategy. Remember, it is almost always easier to prove the value of a low-cost, low-frills option than to justify one that includes all of the bells and whistles. I can cost-justify owning an

automobile that simply runs far more easily than I can cost-justify a new sports car. In working with organizations across a broad range of industries, experience suggests that:

- Short-term results often can turn the opposition around quite quickly.
- What you learn from these systems tends to strengthen the data, process, and functionality of a longer-term solution.
- Advanced features and functions often are not necessary. Keeping things simple is often in the best interest of all involved.

Determining Where Your System Resides

A third business issue relates to whether you build and/or maintain your CRM system and related capabilities internally or outsource. There are a number of factors to consider in making this decision, including:

- *Solution Scope.* Since the term CRM solution could refer to any number of things, this is a valid issue. Your CRM solution could equate to strictly an outbound e-mail capability, or it could be as broad as a multichannel integrated sales, service, and marketing capability that may actually involve many components. In general, the broader the scope of the solution, the greater the value of insourcing.

- *Core Competencies.* The further your organization might be from truly becoming customer-focused, the less the probability of CRM systems development and support being high on your IT group's priority list. Therefore, outsourcing may be an option.

- *Time Horizons.* If you are looking for short-term capabilities due to budgets or other factors, outsourcing can prove to be an efficient means of getting started.

- *IT Resources.* Some organizations may lack internal technology resources altogether, or lack those with adequate experience in managing customer information. To obtain implementation resources, outsourcing may be appropriate. The solution could be brought in-house at some point in the future, provided that resources become available.

These are just a few factors that may impact your decision. The good news is that the alternatives are virtually endless because there are many solutions that can be insourced or outsourced depending on your needs.

Understanding Data Quality

Data is not very exciting and may not be considered a business issue, but without it your CRM strategies and best intentions won't get very far. Data is an absolute critical element of your CRM success. There are a wide range of measures of data quality; the measures you use depends largely on your business applications and related degree of data relevance. Just some of the key data quality measures that you should be monitoring include:

- *Data Coverage.* Coverage refers to the degree to which a particular data field is populated. For example, customers' birth dates would seem on the surface to be a valuable attribute; but if you find that this information is only collected 2 percent of the time, its contribution to customer intelligence is greatly diminished.

- *Data Accuracy.* Coverage alone provides little value. You need to continue to monitor the degree to which your data actually represents

> *"HP believes that customers are ultimately always people, though in the business-to-business arena, that customer relationship is wrapped in much greater complexity. Contacts at a major installed-base account need to be understood in relation to the company they represent, the subsidiary and site they work in, the entitlements they may have in their organizational role, their knowledge of their company and its preferences (as well as their own preferences), and the fact that they may also be consumer customers of HP in their private life."*
>
> —Roger Williams, Hewlett-Packard

reality. Faulty data collection and the inaccuracies introduced as data ages are just two of the challenges to accurate data.

- *Data Precision.* Precision refers to the specificity of the data point. Pinpointing, for instance, that someone's age is 47 can be a great deal more valuable than knowing that individuals are between the ages of 45 and 60.

- *Data Relevance.* You may collect and maintain data that has no value to your CRM efforts. Remember that the objective isn't to gather data for the sake of data, but to build information about the customer. Concentrate on those data points that give you the greatest, most useful insights.

Making Data Accessible

A very obvious related issue is the accessibility of this data to those who can turn it into information and business value. The movement of the 1990s was to empower users with direct access to customer information. What we have learned from this era is a big caveat—direct access to data is fine, as long as the data is in the most practical possible format for specific user applications. Providing an indicator of customer value to customer service representatives is a wonderful idea, but if accessing this data slows down the transactions and actually lessens the customer's service experience, this lack of accessibility slows this wonderful idea to a halt. Building a practical solution involves providing the right information to the right users at the right time, in the right context.

Gaining User Acceptance

Another issue related to users: Are they ready to change the way that they do their jobs and move from a data-poor operating model to a data-driven model? You may develop a wonderful CRM systems environment and may train users on the new software. They may recognize its value. However, they may not be ready to change the way that they operate. It is, after all, much easier to continue to do things the way they have always done them than to change. Change management, therefore, is a key issue, and it is addressed in other chapters of this book. For purposes of this chapter, let's just say that changing users' business practices and standard processes is key to the success of any CRM system.

Before Your Purchase: Advice on Assessing Vendors

New media, new channels, and ongoing convergence of organizational functions continue to spawn new specialized applications. The applications covered in this chapter will continue to "come of age" and eventually merge to form a consolidated CRM capability. As a purchaser or purveyor of CRM technology, it is important to:

- Continue to make technology decisions based on business needs.
- Build or buy the flexibility that is needed to take advantage of this ongoing innovation.

It is a great time to be involved in the development or use of CRM systems, provided that you thrive on continual change and can cope with the volatility in the vendor marketplace. The "Focus" sidebar includes advice on how to work with and/or assess technology firms offering CRM solutions.

Focus: Vendor Volatility— What Can a Client Do?

The current CRM systems marketplace is undergoing continual change. Mergers and acquisitions have become weekly news. Firms are becoming "bigger and better," or becoming bigger simply as a means to remain competitive. You could benefit from these mergers and acquisitions, but in many cases, not without incurring significant short-term risk. You will notice that:

- Many of these acquisitions and mergers are rather large. Some of these firms are in the billion-dollar range.
- These combined companies tend to have services including software, data processing, credit services, brokerage services, and also some form of value-added consulting.

Reasons for the merger and acquisition (M&A) activity include vendors' desires to:

- Realize the operating efficiencies of a larger software or services entity.
- Fuel growth, by basically buying the client relationships as well as the unique assets of another firm.
- Remain competitive; initial M&A activity has spurred additional M&A activity, as firms feel pressured to measure up.
- Meet marketplace needs and increasingly broad applications of technology.

What You Can Expect

If you are a client or prospective client of one of these CRM technology firms, what does all this volatility mean to you? Based on personal experience, my answer would be that the effects of these marketplace changes can range from devastating to extremely advantageous.

To say "devastating" may sound like a somewhat seasoned and sarcastic answer, but there are potential negative impacts on your organization if the vendors you are working with are going through upheaval. Some of these impacts are longer-term in nature and most likely would not be felt for several months—possibly when you are already well into your CRM strategy and implementation. For example, as the technology marketplace shakes out, there are risks of:

- *Staff Turbulence.* Redundant or frustrated staff may leave, and those who remain may be reorganized and no longer assigned to your account.

- *Delays and Confusion.* In the immediate term, some of the vendor's time will be consumed with the internal effects of new ownership. Lack of focus is the biggest danger in the interim period.

- *Product Changes.* Processing centers may be relocated. Some of the "special services" provided by the smaller of the firms may no longer be offered. While product changes could have a very positive long-term impact, they may have some less positive short-term effects on your ability to access data.

- *Service Changes.* Your position may change from being a big fish in a small pond to being a small fish in a big sea.

- *Monopolistic Pricing.* In the longer term, there is the potential of being locked into higher costs or a wider bundle of services than what you had initially bargained for.

The good news is that all of this M&A activity can also provide significant opportunities for new and existing clients. It is important to note, however, that potential benefits cannot be characterized as immediate-term. That is, it is unlikely that you would realize these benefits until several months after a merger or acquisition. Eventual advantageous outcomes for you might be:

- *Improved Products and Services.* In terms of products, more robust CRM system solutions, improved data services, and broader offerings might be available when vendors merge. In terms of services, the combined staff of two or more companies can mean a greater range of experience and expertise that can be brought to bear on your account.

- *One-Stop Shopping.* The new entity can offer a broader range of solutions, or combine solutions into a much more robust product offering.

How to Cope

Realizing these challenges and opportunities, what if you are a client of one of these firms or contracting for work when the merger or acquisition is announced? Here are a few suggestions for how to protect your interests:

1. *Stay informed.* I would encourage this tactic regardless of the vendor scene. Document the details of your internal and outsourced services. Being an informed client can make you a smarter consumer of your vendor's products or services.

2. *Contractually protect yourself.* Think of a contract as an opportunity to protect yourself and control the nature of your relationship with a vendor. Perhaps the vendor has not changed sides or been involved in anything too volatile to date. All the more reason to specify assignment rights, solution specifics, and service levels.

3. *Ask key questions.* Before rushing to judgment about the impact of a merger or acquisition on your account, talk with your vendor's most senior staff. Do so within days of any announced change. If the vendor cannot find time to address your concerns, it may signal a problem. In terms of key questions, find out about the vendor's assessment of the merger or acquisition—how will it be a benefit to you, a client? What might be some of the challenges? If the vendor says it will be "business as usual," you should question further.

4. *Renegotiate.* A merger or acquisition may be an opportunity for you to renegotiate a pending or current contract, particularly if the new organization can support more of your needs.

The potential of these emerging CRM product and service firms is enormous. In the long term, it should equate to stronger service partners with a broader, deeper product mix and service capability, and be more sophisticated for all of us. Just make sure that your vendors' longer-term aspirations can support your more immediate needs.

CHAPTER ELEVEN

MEASURING THE SUCCESS OF YOUR CRM INITIATIVES

You may have picked up this book, having heard that focusing on customer relationships is becoming increasingly critical to business success. You may have read newspaper or other accounts of how organizations such as Hewlett-Packard, Wells Fargo, and Citicorp are focused on customer relationships. This book has also addressed the keys to implementing customer relationship management. But how do you know whether your efforts are really working? Since CRM is such a broad initiative that involves all aspects of your organization, how can you continually measure progress and then tie it to longer-term success? The measurement challenge may be daunting, but it is essential to continued support and success.

Since implementing CRM is time-consuming and requires a significant commitment across your organization, it is essential that you:

- Establish the means of measuring your progress on your CRM initiatives.
- Establish enterprisewide measures of success, and metrics that can be applied to all of your CRM efforts.
- Apply these metrics on an ongoing basis, and use them to guide significant modifications as well as minor adjustments to your plans and to justify continued funding of your CRM initiatives.

This chapter provides an overview of these key measurement principles.

As shown in Figure 11-1, there are five interrelated areas of CRM measurement. Each of these is further explained below.

Measurement of Internal CRM Capabilities

As addressed in Chapter 5, there is an internal transformation process that should drive your CRM practices. This transformation involves your organization's adoption of CRM and the related investment in infrastructure and resources to implement CRM.

The CRM Transformation Map, introduced in Chapter 4 and repeated here in Figure 11-2, is a means of monitoring internal

Figure 11-1. Five aspects of CRM measurement.

1. Internal CRM Capabilities	Have our business focus, organizational structure, customer interaction capabilities, and technology become more supportive of a customer-centric approach?
2. Customer Interactions	How are we supporting the customer experience, across all touchpoints?
3. Customer Dynamics	Have we improved customer acquisition, growth, retention, and reactivation?
4. Operational Efficiencies	Have we saved time and resources through increased system and process efficiencies?
5. Business Metrics	Through our efforts in the areas itemized above, have we increased revenues, decreased costs, and increased competitive differentiation?

improvements in CRM. As stated previously, CRM does not represent a gradual evolution, as your organization should not move through the Transformation Map from one stage to the next. Rather, the goal is to leapfrog from wherever you may be today, to the ideal customer-centric focus (as shown down the right-hand side of the Map).

The best practices in each of the five transformation areas can provide a means of monitoring your success. Additionally, your completion of specific CRM action plan project phases and related efforts are a means of measuring progress over time.

These internal diagnostics provide an immediate and ongoing means of measuring the extent to which your organization is changing and your internal capabilities are improving, which is requisite for achieving any external measures of success. These internal diagnostics also ensure that your CRM investments will be balanced and well coordinated. Organizations often overinvest in some areas; underinvest in others. There may be a heavy focus on technology initiatives, for example, or on e-business capabilities. While these areas are important, a balance is required in order to optimize your total investment. Internal diagnostics therefore

Figure 11-2. CRM Transformation Map.

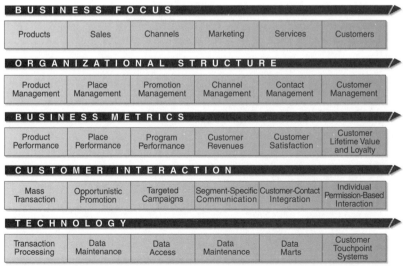

BUSINESS FOCUS					
Products	Sales	Channels	Marketing	Services	Customers

ORGANIZATIONAL STRUCTURE					
Product Management	Place Management	Promotion Management	Channel Management	Contact Management	Customer Management

BUSINESS METRICS					
Product Performance	Place Performance	Program Performance	Customer Revenues	Customer Satisfaction	Customer Lifetime Value and Loyalty

CUSTOMER INTERACTION					
Mass Transaction	Opportunistic Promotion	Targeted Campaigns	Segment-Specific Communication	Customer-Contact Integration	Individual Permission-Based Interaction

TECHNOLOGY					
Transaction Processing	Data Maintenance	Data Access	Data Maintenance	Data Marts	Customer Touchpoint Systems

©1999 Nykamp Consulting Group.

encourage an ongoing balance and a well-rounded strategy.

Measurement of Customer Interactions

A somewhat more customer-focused means of assessing your performance is to continually evaluate your performance relative to the customer interactions identified through the Customer Experience Cycle work outlined in Chapter 3. There are dozens if not hundreds of potential customer interaction opportunities within an organization; the trick is to prioritize them and then focus on optimizing those that have the biggest impact on customer relationships.

A simple customer interaction scorecard can be developed and used as a means of measuring your performance at each point of interaction. A sample of the factors that you might measure on this scorecard is shown in Figure 11-3, with the primary measure being your improvements in performance at each point of interaction. This scorecard should be revisited every two to three months, to understand where progress has been made. The summary statistics recorded at the bottom of this scorecard can spotlight this progress and provide trending information over time.

Improvements in Customer Dynamics

The internal improvements in the areas outlined on the transformation map and the improvements in specific customer interactions should yield related improvements in customer dynamics. These dynamics can include customer acquisition, customer growth and development, customer retention, and customer reactivation. These are the measures with which we are all very familiar because they are the goals of many of our sales, service, and marketing efforts.

- Customer acquisition improvements may relate to increasing the targeting and related response rates or conversion rates of acquisition efforts, or acquiring more valuable or more loyal customers.
- Customer growth and development improvements may relate to increased cross-sell of specific products, increased

Figure 11-3. Sample customer interaction scorecard.

Interaction Opportunity	Past Performance	Current Performance	Importance to Customer Relationship	Improvement Priority
1. Customer e-mails a product-related complaint to customer service.	2	3	3	High
2. Customer calls product support regarding a product feature or function.	3	3	2	Low
3. Customer subscribes to a savings alert e-newsletter.	3	3	2	Low
4. Customer visits our website three times within a week.	1	1	2	Medium
5. Customer receives three renewal notices and does not respond.	1	2	3	Medium
6. Customer cancels a subscription via toll-free # or automated voice-recognition unit.	2	2	2	Medium
7. Customer's order is delayed due to an out-of-stock situation.	1	2	3	High
8. Customer receives his or her first order.	2	3	2	Low
9. Customer does not make a purchase within a nine-month period.	2	2	3	High

Key: 3= High; 2 = Medium; 1 = Low.

profitability of sales to existing accounts, or improved upsell ratios in a call center or online.

- Customer retention improvements may relate to increased customer satisfaction with your online help features or offline call center, creation of loyalty programs for your most valuable customers, or improved response time to customer complaints.

- Customer reactivation improvements may relate to increased performance of any win-back marketing campaigns or direct sales efforts.

You may find that your loyalty program is focused 70 percent on retention and 30 percent on acquisition. A cross-sell program in a call center may be focused 80 percent on penetration, 20 percent on retention. A new customer information management system may be more evenly split between acquisition, penetration, retention, and reactivation. You should map all of your CRM initiatives to these customer metrics and also identify their relative areas of focus. There are two related points to keep in mind when you do so:

1. *Use universal diagnostics across all areas of your organization.* The challenge within many organizations is the lack of standard definitions or measurements of success. Departments and divisions are often guilty of "cherry picking" those measures that paint their initiatives in the most positive light. Different areas of the organization may report on contact rates, response rates, conversion rates, close rates, gross sales, or net margins. While these measures may all be relevant, the divergence between groups and initiatives can become confusing. The lack of standard measures will unfortunately prevent your organization from understanding the true impact of all of your CRM efforts.

2. *Recognize the interdependencies.* Another common and often fatal flaw is the failure to recognize or acknowledge the interdependencies between various CRM initiatives. For example:

   – A marketing group may demonstrate how an improved targeting model has improved response, without acknowledging the related investment the organization has made in improved data collection.
   – An inbound call center may attribute increased close rates to recent testing and fine-tuning of its call scripts. It may fail to acknowledge, or may not even realize, the more stringent list qualification work that was simultaneously being pursued by the marketing department.
   – A sales force may not realize or may not acknowledge that its increased conversion rates are a result of a combination

of other internal initiatives, ranging from improved targeting of marketing efforts to tighter lead qualification in the call center.

It is obviously essential that all areas of the organization understand how their efforts fit within the bigger picture. Failure to acknowledge the interdependencies can lead to the downfall of your efforts, as the structures and systems and departments that supported your success could be called into question. Take a look around you: What are all of the essential elements of your success?

Improvements in Operations

Many of the internal areas of transformation are going to result in improvements in core operational efficiencies. These may include cost reductions in data collection, maintenance or access, or fulfillment; the identification of fraud or other problems; and increased overall integration of core business processes.

These operational improvements, while often overshadowed by the "curb appeal" of customer dynamics, are also measurable and substantial. Many customer data warehousing initiatives are justified strictly on the basis of increased data maintenance efficiencies. New call center technology may be similarly justified on the basis of reduced staffing expenses.

Bottom-Line Business Metrics

Finally, the improvements in customer dynamics and in operations result in measurable changes in bottom-line business metrics. There are really only three bottom-line measures of success for CRM or any other business initiative:

- Increased revenues
- Decreased costs
- Increased competitive differentiation

Your CRM livelihood as a client or vendor depends on your ability to tie all of your initiatives and resulting improvements to these measures. Everyone within your organization may understand that improving media selection, collecting data online, or accessing customer data in a call center can have an impact on your bottom line. Everyone within your organization certainly would understand how improving customer acquisition, increasing customer retention, or increasing customer penetration could have an impact on your bottom line. It is important, however, to quantify the size of that impact.

While this sounds like a logical conclusion, I would submit that most CRM initiatives that are being pursued today have not been held to these measurement principles. What seems to be the more common approach today is one of agreement-in-principle. Since CRM seems to be the "talk of the town" across many organizations, a wide range of sizable technology, marketing, sales, service, and organizational proposals are escalated to senior management. Since senior management embraces the CRM concept in general, the first five to ten proposals receive wholesale approval because they all demonstrate some positive impact on customer relationships. After several more CRM projects are proposed, the question of relative importance may be posed.

Rather than beginning with the initiatives that may come to mind first, or with whatever the first vendor in the door may offer, broad-scale quantification of potential return on investment must be pursued. Take each of your potential initiatives and tie them to projected, quantified improvements in customer dynamics (e.g., acquisition, retention, penetration, and reactivation). Next, determine and quantify how improvements in these dynamics impact revenue, costs, and competitive differentiation. Completing this planning work prior to any investments in technology, marketing, analytics, infrastructure, or organizational changes will enable you to prioritize the relative importance of each of your potential initiatives.

If your CRM efforts are not held to these bottom-line standards today, it is safe to assume that they will be in the near future. Your initial efforts may have been funded because they were such obvious necessities, or because of the excitement or corporate good-citizenship that these efforts entailed. However, the ongoing funding and support of increasingly large CRM investments and related corporate change initiatives will require demonstrable bottom-line success stories.

Focus: The Importance of the Total Customer Experience for HP

The following excerpts are from Hewlett-Packard CEO Carly Fiorina, speaking on the importance of one of the main initiatives she has instituted.

"Customers expect a superior total customer experience from HP that adds value to them in the way they define it. Customer interactions take place at many different times and in many different ways—including the way they become aware of us and how we can help them when they buy from us, when they use our products and services, and when they seek our help and support.

"Our customers tell us that we need to spend more energy on understanding and improving the sum total of our efforts. The sum of all our customers' experiences with HP needs to increase their loyalty to our company.

"As a company, we should know our customers and their organizations as well as we know our own. We need to remember what they tell us and act based on their feedback. When we interact with them, no matter the medium, we represent all of HP.

"I'll hold my managers accountable for understanding the total customer experience in their markets and assuring they meet their goals. And we'll actively identify and remove organizational barriers that inhibit our focus on the total customer experience. I expect my managers to do the same in their organizations. . . . It's the job of every employee to assume responsibility to contribute to our customers' ultimate success, as they perceive it."

Where Do You Go from Here?

I have outlined the ins and outs of what is involved in CRM intiatives, and the best practices that will hopefully guide you on your way to success. The case studies that follow are intended to provide real-life examples of organizations that are learning valuable lessons while implementing CRM initiatives. (The identities and details of these initiatives have been masked for confidentiality purposes.)

To summarize these valuable lessons:

- *CRM initiatives need to be driven by business goals and objectives.* Pursuing CRM because it is currently in vogue will not result in meaningful initiatives or measurable results. Pursuing CRM as a technology will never drive business success. Rather, decide why your organization should pursue CRM, and quantify your goals for CRM initiatives prior to launching CRM infrastructure or process-improvement projects.

- *CRM requires aggressive, ongoing organization and planning.* Gaining the customer differential will not happen on its own accord; you will need to put the processes and plans in place to make it happen. Industry research points to lack of planning as the number one reason CRM initiatives fail. My experience in working with clients in organizations both large and small confirms this finding. These plans need to span departmental boundaries and include all functional areas of the organization. Figuring out how to structure and then work more effectively together as an organization is actually often a valuable side-benefit of these initiatives.

- *Balance your planning with action.* While you could continue to read a plethora of CRM how-to books and attend a never-ending array of CRM conferences in locations near and far, I would encourage you to jump in and get started. CRM becomes far too difficult and overwhelming when overanalyzed. While failure to plan is most prevalent, overdoing it on the planning front can stymie some of the most intelligent and otherwise successful organizations.

  Start small, and start with the basics. Some of the seemingly simplest, foundational steps can be the most important.

- *Stick with it!* In addition to encouraging you to "just do it," I need to encourage you to stick with it. The buzzwords are bound to change, and a portion of the technology crowd is bound to move on to the next big systems "thing" over the next couple of years. Your decision will be to abandon CRM and move with them, or to continue to invest in and reap benefits from your newly honed CRM capabilities and practices.

If you think that your organization will be one to walk away, you might want to think twice about even starting any major CRM work at this point. As demonstrated throughout this book, realizing success with CRM will take time; far more time than business buzzwords and hot trends will remain. Obviously, I would like to see you all succeed; I would therefore encourage you to stick with it.

My final words of advice are that you start somewhere, start small, and, of course, start soon. The customer differential can be the source to your sustained success.

CHAPTER TWELVE

CASE STUDY: CLOTHES UNLIMITED

Situation Overview

Clothes Unlimited (CU) is a very large, publicly held clothing retail and manufacturing company that consists of several of this nation's leading apparel marketers and brands. Well-known CU holdings include:

- Delphi's, a chain of moderately priced department stores
- Sally Fourth, a leading women's sportswear brand
- Kimmerling, a leading women's fashion and career wear brand
- Wanda's Wardrobe, a retail store and mail-order catalog business appealing to girls in their teens and early twenties
- Connor's Closet, a retail store and mail-order catalog business appealing to boys in their teens and early twenties

- The Baby's Room, a chain of retail stores carrying everything for baby, including home décor as well as clothing

CU grew significantly since the company's founder, Horace Christoff, opened the first Delphi's store more than fifty years ago. CU's combined retail presence now canvasses the United States, Canada, and Latin America. Wanda's Wardrobe catalog, a leader in teen fashion, just expanded to the Asia-Pacific market as well as Europe. CU's combined operations total to more than 1,000 retail outlets and over $1 billion in annualized revenues. Figure 12-1, taken from a recent annual report, summarizes the CU enterprise.

CU entities operate fairly independently; they each have their own corporate headquarters, manufacturing and operations facilities, and distribution and service networks. This independent operating structure had been positioned with the investment community as essential for supporting and maintaining the unique nature of each brand. Internally, however, there were ongoing talks of consolidation and centralization. These talks had never really materialized in the past, until most recently, when they seemed to take on a more serious tone.

Figure 12-1. Clothes Unlimited: enterprise overview.

Entity	Retail Locations	Regions
Delphi's	272	United States, Canada, United Kingdom, Sweden
Wanda's Wardrobe	488	United States, Canada, Latin America, Japan (catalog only), China (catalog only)
Connor's Closet	164	United States, Canada
The Baby's Room	290	United States, Canada, Latin America
Sally Fourth	Distribution network; 22 U.S. outlet stores	United States, Canada, United Kingdom, Germany, Sweden, Netherlands, Switzerland
Kimmerling	Distribution network; 16 U.S. outlet stores	United States, Canada, Latin America, Hungary, Ireland

Each of the divisional presidents reported up to Christine Christoff, CU's chief executive since 1998 and daughter of the company founder. The company experienced significant growth since Christine officially took the helm, and many of her initiatives were very well received by investors. At one annual meeting, Christine announced the following series of initiatives for the coming year:

- Consolidating warehouse operations
- Increasing same-store sales over 10 percent, per year per store, across all divisions
- Closing unprofitable stores
- Moving more aggressively into European markets with Wanda's Wardrobe and The Baby's Room
- Expanding direct marketing, primarily through e-commerce and other web-based initiatives
- Focusing on data warehousing, and using systems and data to drive marketing and service capabilities, as well as product development

Internally, there were a wide range of opinions on each of these initiatives. Christine instituted a comprehensive communications program that included a series of companywide meetings using teleconferencing to reach all of the various CU locations. The communications effort continued for thirty days before the divisions began to formally act on these initiatives.

All of the items on Christine's list represented significant new initiatives for CU. Most of them entailed cooperation if not consolidation across the divisions. Multidivisional taskforces and subgroups were formed to manage each of these initiatives. Many of the members of these groups were dedicated as full-time resources to the work at hand. This case study focuses on the last but not least of these initiatives—data warehousing—and the work of CU's Data Warehousing Taskforce.

The Data Warehousing Taskforce

The core Data Warehousing Taskforce initially consisted of twelve members from CU's various divisions. As shown in Figure 12-2, there were ten IT professionals and two business professionals in the initial group. Each of them was assigned a role on the taskforce based on their previous experience, expertise, and interests.

CRM Implementation

One of the first tasks of the Data Warehousing Taskforce was to develop an appropriate charter. Bill Reilly was an advocate of project charters. He preached that this charter would define and drive all taskforce efforts over the next twelve to twenty-four months. The development of this charter statement also gave the group an

Figure 12-2. CU Data Warehousing Taskforce.

Member	Title	Taskforce Role
Jim Hayes	CIO, Delphi's	Leader
Juanita Gonzales	VP Technology Applications, Delphi's	Applications Lead
Victor Korn	Senior Programmer, Wanda's	Development Lead
Stephen Cary	Analyst, Wanda's	Analyst, Discovery Process
Sue Pollack	Systems Manager, Connor's	Analyst, Discovery Process
Sindu Wajami	DBA, Connor's	Analyst, Discovery Process
Kevin O'Farrell	Technical Architect, The Baby's Room	Development Team
Karen Furth	Applications Specialist, The Baby's Room	Development Team
Mary O'Donnell	Analyst, Sally Fourth	Analyst, Discovery Process
Joel Stephenson	Analyst, Kimmerling	Analyst, Discovery Process
Bill Reilly	VP Marketing, Delphi's	Business Representative
Sren Sojak	Customer Service Manager, Connor's	Business Representative

initial chance to work together and get to know each other. The charter that the group developed is as follows:

> *The mission of the CU Data Warehousing Taskforce is to consolidate, cleanse, and maintain Clothes Unlimited's mission-critical data for business purposes.*

Some taskforce members wanted to qualify this charter significantly; they felt that the following qualifiers were missing and may divert their efforts:

- The data warehousing efforts should be focused on customer data and customer interactions with CU.
- The data warehousing business focus should be on CRM.
- The data warehousing efforts should initially meet the needs of the U.S. and Canadian markets.
- The taskforce should only be held responsible for defining solutions, not actually developing them.

These qualifiers were voted down because the team collectively felt that keeping the charter broad would allow them the flexibility that they may need. They agreed, however, that qualifiers may be added to their mission following an extensive discovery process.

The Discovery Process

Within the taskforce, a team of five were assigned to lead an extensive discovery process. This effort involved a great deal of information gathering over a ten-month period. Their goal was to understand the data, processing, and systems maintained by each of the CU divisions, and that included a combination of new and legacy systems and a variety of other divisional IT projects.

The five business analysts quickly became overwhelmed and requested additional resources. Six IT contractors were added to the internal team. The discovery team had identified a total of twenty-seven core systems that should be evaluated and considered within the scope of this discovery process. These could all serve as potential source systems for the data warehouse.

One of the biggest challenges that the discovery team faced was the lack of consistent, reliable documentation on existing systems and processes. For some systems, no one other than the original system architect had a thorough understanding of its contents or core functions. In some cases, this original system expert was no longer with the company. In other cases, this individual had been assigned other responsibilities and therefore lacked the availability to work with the team and a working familiarity with the system.

A related complexity was that all of the divisions had numerous active systems initiatives and projects under development. These ranged from enterprise resource planning (ERP) implementations, to point-of-sale (POS) system installations or enhancements, to marketing database efforts, to divisional data warehousing initiatives. Therefore, their view of the current situation was subject to significant change.

After ten exhausting months of work, the discovery process was nowhere near complete. Many of the team members were working around the clock, with no end in sight. The team of analysts and contractors were frustrated, and two of the original team members had left for other CU projects. Jim Hayes, the data warehousing lead who had not been very involved in this discovery work due to other Wanda's Wardrobe project commitments, tried to encourage the team. He suggested that they develop an initial findings document, with recommendations that could be brought to senior management to secure ongoing and additional funding to complete the discovery process work and actually begin the data warehousing efforts.

The team welcomed this suggestion because it provided them with a relatively short-term manageable goal. They spent the next eight weeks consolidating all of their notes, reports, and other documentation that they had received from the various system owners. The paperwork alone was overwhelming. They decided that the best approach was to remove themselves from the details and focus on key findings. Abandoning all of their paperwork that was piled in an otherwise unoccupied cubicle, they met to discuss the overarching findings of all of their work.

Many of their initial observations and statements reflected

their frustration much more than their findings. After some time, they were able to begin to itemize and categorize their thoughts as follows:

Systems

- We have a confusing array of tools and technologies across CU, and even within the divisions. We need corporate standards for hardware, software, and related applications.

- Most systems are poorly documented, if documented at all. This has caused many problems for us on this project, and for others. Documentation standards are therefore also needed.

- Some IT functions, such as data processing, should potentially be centralized. Some of our divisions have strong existing capabilities, but some do not. Some outsource and probably overpay for these services.

Data Warehousing Project

- We need to define a much tighter charter for what we are trying to do. We should initially limit ourselves to one division, one country—something less than everything.

- We need to define how this project might relate to existing divisional data warehousing efforts. Some of these projects are much further along than ours. Should those efforts be shut down, or should we piggyback on their efforts?

- We need a business-focused charter. We need a business sponsor for our efforts—possibly someone from marketing, service, research, or another functional unit.

- We need tighter budgets for our efforts. (According to its internal accounting standards, the Data Warehousing Taskforce had spent more than $1.8 million over the last year and lacked a deliverable.)

These findings were presented to Hayes, who until this point had not understood the extent of the team's frustration. He augmented their ideas with a few of his own and prepared the presentation for senior management. He included much of the detailed documentation that his team had prepared.

Needless to say, the meeting did not go well. Hayes tried his best to present the work of his Data Warehousing Taskforce as a foundation for future deliverables as well as broader IT initiatives. He tried to assure senior management that the tangible results of their efforts would come to light in the next six to twelve months. CU's Corporate CIO, Hugh Franks, tried to come to Hayes's aid, to no avail.

Senior management cut the project from its upcoming fiscal year budget. Some commented on the misuse of valuable IT staff that could have served key roles within the divisions. Hayes, now frustrated and angered by senior management's reaction to the team's hard work, had to report the decision back to the team members.

Conclusions

Hayes personally took some of the responsibility for the downfall of the Data Warehousing Taskforce. The rest of the blame was placed on senior management for its shortsightedness in cutting this project.

The taskforce was actually relieved by the news of project discontinuation. Each of the team members knew that the project, as it stood, was doomed even if Hayes had secured another twelve months of funding. Team members could now go back to their responsibilities in their respective divisions. None of them wanted to worry about corporate initiatives ever again. The company, after all, was built on a foundation of independence.

Lessons Learned

It would seem that there are a wide variety of business opportunities to consolidate, analyze, and apply data from across the Clothes Unlimited organization. Just a few of the CRM-related applications could include general customer behavioral analysis, product purchase analysis, cross-divisional shopping behavior analyses, customer segmentation, and lifetime value analysis (LTV), as well as the accessibility of customer data in CU's soon-to-be-centralized call centers. This is above and beyond the technical efficiencies of having common system standards, shared system licenses, and potentially shared processes and applications. All of this makes wonderful sense.

However, there are several lessons that we can learn from CU's foray into data warehousing. Any organization's CRM success depends on its ability to avoid such costly mistakes and take away these lessons learned:

- *A technology project always requires a very specific business charter.* The goals of some of these projects could be as commonplace as replacing a system to increase throughput, or standardizing an operating platform in order to reduce software licensing and training expenses. The goals of other projects may be loftier, if focused on improving business decision making or customer relationship management. Nonetheless, these project goals need to be specific and measurable.

- *Technology projects cannot drive changes in the business.* Business issues, rather, need to drive technology needs and technology projects.

- *The scope of any data warehousing project can quickly get out of hand.* Safeguards need to be put in place to prevent this.

- *Building systems to support CRM capabilities is a difficult business.* Whether you are talking about marketing, sales, service, or other functional areas, a CRM initiative typically involves a wide range of both organizational and systems dependencies, any of which could prove problematic.

CHAPTER THIRTEEN

CASE STUDY: FIRST CENTURY FINANCIAL

Situation Overview

First Century Financial is a large national banking and financial services concern. First Century was formed through the merger of First Financial, Century FiServ, and seventeen other smaller regional banks and investment firms in 1998. With this consolidation and growth, the scope of First Century's services grew to include those shown in Figure 13-1.

Over the last eighteen months, the firm's core operations were consolidated and centralized. Best-of-breed departments were formed from the various entities in the following areas:

- Business strategy and management
- Advertising and marketing
- Public relations
- Branch operations

Figure 13-1. First Century's services.

Consumer	
Checking Accounts	Home Equity Loans
Savings Accounts	Credit Lines
Money Market Accounts	Mortgages
IRAs	Auto and Homeowner's Insurance
Credit Cards	Personal Investment Advice
Business	
Small Business	*Commercial*
Deposit Accounts	Retirement Plans
Credit Accounts	Real Estate Financing
Merchant Services	Business Financing
Payroll Services	Cash Management
Credit Cards	International Trade Services

- Information technology
- Accounting and legal
- Product development and management (six new core product divisions)

First Century's consolidated customer database spanned thirty-four states. The company had more than 27 million active residential and business accounts, and more than 700 branch offices, 1,000 ATMs, and 20,000 personnel with which to serve its burgeoning customer base.

With all of this growth and consolidation also came inevitable challenges. Perhaps the largest and the least expected was general customer concern and backlash in response to the mergers and emergence of First Century as an enormous, centralized financial services entity. Unfortunately, the media spurred on much of this concern. Several highly publicized stories covered the impact this merger had on customers. Much of the news coverage suggested that those in the know were fleeing to smaller, regional banks like the bank they "used to know." Needless to say, all of this press had a very negative impact on First Century's ability to actually achieve economies of scale. Management was too busy just trying to maintain the norm and retain existing customer accounts.

Dozens of internal groups were aggressively working on all aspects of the new merger—from systems consolidation efforts to product consolidation to branch redistribution. Unfortunately, the customer relations aspect of the merger became so visible that a sizable taskforce was formed with the overarching objective of improving customer relationships. This taskforce was staffed with some of the strongest strategic thinkers within First Century, including strategists from operations, marketing, public relations, information technology, and product management.

CRM Implementation
Scoping

The Customer Relationship Taskforce (CRT) realized the overwhelming size of its undertaking. The team hired a consulting firm to assist in the initial scoping and planning effort. CRT members dedicated significant time to this effort, as they realized that they were working with the most visible black eye that First Century had received since the taskforce's formation.

Within an initial phase one scope of customer relationship management and improvement, the taskforce turned its attention to the following areas:

- Individual consumers: First Century's consumer business was much larger, and the potential impact of the merger was much more significant on the consumer market than the business market.
- All customer interactions (e.g., sales, service, marketing, and PR) across all channels (e.g., branches, ATMs, call centers, and the Internet).
- All consumer product and service groups across all of the acquired banks' regions.

While this was a tremendously broad scope, the team realized that it could not exclude any of these aspects of the customer experience.

Situation Assessment

The group then embarked on a process of assessing First Century's current CRM capabilities and practices. There were two aspects of this assessment; the first being an external assessment of the customer's experience with First Century, and the second being an internal evaluation of First Century's capabilities.

Customer Experience. The taskforce conducted what it termed a customer point-of-contact audit as a means of identifying and quantifying all of First Century's interactions with customers. Early into this effort, the team recognized that the frequency and nature of these interactions varied considerably by customer segment. Optimally, the taskforce wanted to conduct an audit for each of eight consumer segments. However, due to time and budget constraints, it conducted this audit across the consumer business as a whole.

The taskforce began with recognition of the consumer purchasing process for First Century's products and services. Past research suggested that beyond the standard checking and savings products, the education stage of the cycle was critical to the success of most sales efforts and that educating consumers had to be supported across all channels and media.

The team continued this effort by evaluating the quantity, nature, and quality of current customer contacts across all channels and media. This resulted in a list of more than 200 distinct types of inbound and outbound contacts across:

- Branches and the interactions with various departments (e.g., tellers, personal bankers) within the branch
- Call centers and customer service phone centers
- First Century's website
- ATMs

- Direct marketing communications
- Advertising
- Corporate communications/PR

The taskforce assessed the importance of each contact, First Century's current support of each contact, and a related priority for improvement. This resulted in a shortlist of eleven types of interactions that deserved the most immediate attention, as shown in Figure 13-2.

Figure 13-2. High-priority consumer interaction scoreboard.

When a Customer...
. . . requests investment product performance information via the call center
. . . attends one of the branch's "Investing Made Easy" seminars
. . . escalates a service issue to a branch manager
. . . requests a new account kit via the web or call center
. . . accesses the Personal Investment Planner online
. . . receives recommendations from the Personal Investment Planner application
. . . sends a service complaint via e-mail
. . . discontinues online banking activity
. . . receives a notice regarding increased service fees that will affect the customer's banking activity
. . . withdraws an unusually large amount from any account without a subsequent deposit into another First Century product
. . . meets with a personal banker to discuss investment options

These key interaction opportunities would require the most immediate business process and systems reengineering in order to better support customers' needs and First Century's business.

First Century's Capabilities. The second aspect of the CRT's situation assessment focused on First Century's overarching CRM capabilities. Evaluating customer interactions provided some insights as to the systems and infrastructure needed to support improved customer relationships. After much discussion, the taskforce placed First Century on the CRM transformation map (see Figure 13-3), then spent a considerable amount of time talking about the ideal—talking about CRM best practices and how they would apply to First Century.

Gap Analysis
By the sixth month, the taskforce was prepared to begin to identify gaps in the company's current capabilities—gaps that were hindering or at minimum were not optimizing the customer's experience. The general feeling of the group was that there was no middle of the road; if you were not helping a customer relationship grow, you were hindering it.

Gaps were identified in the five categories highlighted in Figure 13-3. Some of the most notable gaps were explained as follows:

Business Focus
- We do not have common definition of CRM, or common CRM goals and objectives related to customer acquisition, development, and retention. Most goals are by product line and region.
- We do not have a good understanding of our customers and who they are. We are relying primarily on preacquisition notions.
- We are no longer a customer-focused organization. With the mergers and acquisitions, we have become very focused on ourselves and have forgotten about our customers.

Organizational Structure
- The current organization is a mess. The existing management teams are all trying to protect their own turf and jostling for position.
- There has been tremendous turnover in customer service, with the relocation of many of our service centers. The new centralized centers may be larger and higher-tech, but they may come across as extremely impersonal.

Figure 13-3. First Century's Transformation Mapping.

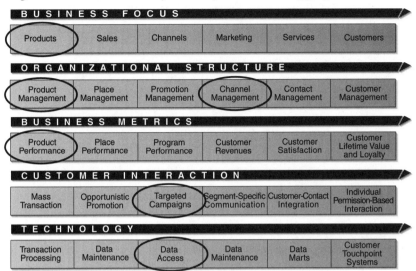

©1999 Nykamp Consulting Group.

Business Metrics

- We do not have any standard measures of success other than what is reported to Wall Street. There are no measures related to customer performance or customer value.

Customer Interaction

- Our focus is primarily on outbound marketing campaigns that are typically driven by the product groups or regions.
- There is very little coordination, if any, between these campaigns.
- We need to begin to develop segment-specific contact strategies and operationalize those into our marketing plans.

Technology

- We have just begun to develop a centralized customer data warehouse. Consolidating all of our customer data in order to efficiently centralize marketing and more appropriately service customers will likely require another year. We need some short-term means of coordinating our efforts.

- We need to ensure that the data warehouse team understands companywide needs for customer data.

- We need to begin to look at a means of dynamically providing relevant customer information to the customer service and operations representatives, so that they can have the best possible interaction with each customer who calls.

- We need to somehow coordinate all of the various Internet and e-banking initiatives so that they are moving forward with us rather than moving in their own direction.

The Customer Relationship Taskforce was once again reminded of the size and scope of this CRM undertaking, and the related depth and breadth of the gaps that currently existed within First Century. Was it any wonder that there were customer concerns, complaints, and attrition?

CRM Plan Development

The CRT also realized that it could not begin to address all of these issues. Taskforce members had identified a number of customer interactions that required retooling. Relatedly, they had developed a list of broad organizational capabilities and infrastructures that should be addressed. They also realized that many of these initiatives had other dependencies. Therefore, their next step was to further cut down this list and identify a manageable subset that should be pursued over the coming three to six months.

This prioritization was not easy. Everyone seemed to have conflicting opinions as to which initiatives were most important and which should be pursued first and why. The arguments often became very heated and in some cases unproductive. Finally, one of the members of the taskforce suggested an objective means of prioritizing the initiatives. It was a simple scoring system that she had seen applied to this type of business planning in the past. The score sheet basically asked each taskforce member to score each of the initiatives based on feasibility, time, cost, potential return, and also potential dependencies. Scores were then averaged from across the group, and the following initiatives were identified for phase I implementation:

1. Develop a common definition of CRM across the organization.

2. Create an understanding of our consumer customer base. Who are our customers? How do interactions vary by consumer customer segment? Begin some centralized marketing planning efforts. Form a taskforce to share current practices and, over time, share marketing planning cycles.

3. Standardize the handling and escalation process on all customer complaints.

4. Develop a turnkey follow-up process to follow the fulfillment of new account kits.

5. Identify and communicate the overarching business needs that should be supported by the customer data warehouse.

The group stopped short of documenting subsequent phases or initiatives because it anticipated that these initial efforts would have a major impact on the next series of initiatives.

At this point, the CRT's initial effort was nearing completion. The team packaged its planning work into a presentation for senior management. Team members decided to include some general educational CRM slides in their deck, to begin to demonstrate the breadth and significance of CRM for First Century management.

The presentation went extremely well. Senior managers were very pleased by the work that the taskforce had accomplished, although they also felt somewhat overwhelmed by all of the work that lay ahead. Each member of the CRT offered to be a pivotal member of one of the phase one subgroups that resulted from their recommendations. These initiatives were formally launched as projects, with dedicated resources, project plans, and group operating policies to ensure timely success. At the same time, these projects had centralized reporting to ensure coordination and synergies.

Conclusions

The phase one groups were all successful in accomplishing their goals. There were inevitable snags in the process, turf wars, misunderstandings, and difficult group dynamics. Nonetheless, they persevered and within six months could proudly point to their accomplishments.

The initial efforts—largely communication, education, and closer collaboration within the combined First Century conglomerate—provided a solid foundation for future CRM phases and initiatives.

Lessons Learned

First Century's progress to date can serve as an example to many other large, complex organizations. The success of its Customer Relationship Taskforce suggests the following:

- Implementing CRM broadly across a large, complex organization can be an overwhelming undertaking. It is critical to plan longer-term, but then prioritize and focus on a handful of short-term efforts.
- Frameworks, scorecards, maps, and templates can provide objectivity and common definition to complex business challenges.
- Communication, education, and collaboration on CRM thinking and implementation are critical to your success.

CHAPTER FOURTEEN

CASE STUDY: INTECH COMMUNICATIONS INTERNATIONAL

Situation Overview

InTech Communications International develops and operates communications groups in the United States, Eastern Europe, and several other international markets. The holding company's offerings include international toll call services, long-distance services, wireless cable, and paging systems (see Figure 14-1). The company grew quickly over the past ten years, expanding its footprint in the United States and abroad, and also expanding its service offerings largely through an aggressive acquisition strategy. The company's last fiscal year revenues topped $900 million, making the publicly held company a Wall Street darling. W. Brooks Rice, founder and CEO, owns a reported 18 percent of the company.

InTech is pursuing seven key strategic initiatives, ranging from its introduction of a revolutionary new digital calling plan in the U.S. market to its entrance into the European Internet service provider (ISP) arena.

Figure 14-1. InTech's holdings.

Company/Subsidiary	Products	Market
InTech EuroCom (100%)	International toll call services, paging, PCS/cellular	United Kingdom, Belgium, Austria, Romania, Russia, Germany, Hungary Czech Republic, Ireland
InTech Online (100%)	Internet ISP	United Kingdom, Belgium, Austria, Romania, Russia, Germany, Hungary, Czech Republic, Ireland
InTech Wireless TV (100%)	Wireless cable TV services, wireless TV product manufacturing (e.g., satellite dishes, receivers, transmitters, remote control devices)	United Kingdom, Belgium, Austria, Romania, Russia, Germany, Hungary, Czech Republic, Ireland
ITM Communications (100%)	Long distance, paging, PCS/cellular service	United States, Canada
NewsNet TV (40%)	Cable news channel	United States, Europe, Asia

Sales and Marketing Overview

One of the keys to InTech's rapid expansion and growth is said to be the company's aggressive yet humorous advertising campaigns. These advertising efforts have been largely through broad-reach media—television, radio, billboards, and sponsorships. The company's "How Do You InTech?" message and lyrics have appealed to a wide range of the public. The company has also found that much of what worked in the United States could also be applied and aired internationally. This has enabled InTech to recognize significant economies of scale. InTech made some minor changes to its campaigns over time, but held the message and lyrics constant to reinforce the brand. Its advertising agency won numerous awards for these campaigns three years running.

Broad-reach media worked well for the products and services that had broad-scale appeal; namely, long-distance and standard cellular services. The company found, however, that it faced challenges penetrating the market for specialty paging, cellular, and digital packages. These products had less of a universal appeal, as their price-points, features, and benefits are primarily targeted to business applications. This was true in the U.S. as well as in Canadian and European markets. Significant increases in advertising spent on these product categories did not result in incremental customer acquisition or revenues.

InTech's marketers held a related series of brainstorming meetings with Apollo, the company's worldwide advertising agency of record. They jointly concluded that there was a need for more targeted media for these more targeted product families— namely, paging and cellular.

These discussions soon led to discussions about database marketing and the need for a consolidated customer database. This was all new for the general marketing executives at InTech; it was also new terrain for the Apollo account team that had always supported broad-reach advertising. Needless to say, all involved found the discussion to be somewhat confusing as well as disarming. Most of those in the room had an elementary understanding of what targeted marketing and targeted media and marketing databases were all about. None of them could speak definitively.

The action items resulting from this meeting were as follows.

Apollo's Action Plan
- Identify agency resources with greater familiarity with database marketing and direct mail.
- Create media plans and related materials for targeted campaigns for both NeverDown Paging (U.S.) and BizPack Cellular (U.S., Canada, Belgium).
- Identify potential reductions in broad-reach media spending to cover these campaign expenditures.

InTech's Action Plan
- Direct InTech's internal information technology (IT) group to develop a consolidated, relational, worldwide customer and prospect database that could be used to support these initial campaigns and all future targeted efforts.

InTech and its advertising agency set preliminary targets of implementing their first targeted campaign for BizPack in three months; NeverDown in four months.

CRM Implementation

Two parallel paths then ensued; the first being the marketing planning process led by the agency, and the second being the technology development initiative led by InTech's IT group.

Marketing Planning

The InTech worldwide marketing team was naturally involved in the marketing planning efforts because it was much more accustomed to working with the agency and much more accustomed to planning marketing efforts than planning systems. After several weeks of planning work, Apollo presented to InTech's internal team the following recommendations:

1. *Do not reduce the general advertising budget to accommodate these targeted programs.* The Apollo representatives noted that any reduction in general advertising spending could have a detrimental effect on general image and brand awareness. They estimated the incremental budget for the initial targeted programs should be $1.7 million (US$). The direct mail test plan for NeverDown Paging should:

- Include two format tests using standard and oversize packages.
- Include three creative tests, varying the letter copy and key components.
- Target current customers who spend over $200 on long distance per month.
- Target one or two prospect lists.

2. *BizPack Cellular should be tested with a combination of outbound telemarketing, direct mail, and e-mail.* Similarly, there were a number of different test recommendations:

- Use two alternate telemarketing scripts, one focused on availability, the second on productivity.
- Use three different creative approaches on the direct mail, varying the letter copy and key components.
- Use two different versions of e-mail copy, an aggressive and a less aggressive version.

These recommendations on how to market the NeverDown and BizPack services were discussed briefly and then accepted by the InTech team. Development of the various components and purchase of media began. Weekly status reports kept everyone on top of all of this activity.

Technology Development

InTech's marketing team was far less involved in the technology planning aspects of this initiative. It deferred to InTech's internal IT group to handle the development of a consolidated, relational, worldwide customer and prospect database that could be used to support these initial campaigns and all future targeted efforts.

In doing so, the marketing team intended to follow InTech's internal IT project launch standards by creating a scope-of-work document. Marketing located the standard scope-of-work template on the corporate intranet and was surprised to find that it was fourteen pages long and pressed for details that InTech's marketers were not prepared to even begin to answer, much less document.

Roger DeBoer, the most operational member of the InTech marketing team, was assigned the task of reviewing the document. He concluded that an IT project launch necessitated the following:

- *Project Objectives.* The first requirement was documentation on what the project was intended to achieve (e.g., cost savings? other efficiencies? increased revenues? other organizational benefits?).
- *Needs Summary.* This synopsis would identify what the business team felt was needed (e.g., a new system? a new process? more data? faster service? streamlining across the board?).

- *Business Case.* A cost/benefit analysis would include estimated project costs (both external and internal) and projected benefits over five years.
- *Implications.* Any organizational, technical, or other effects that this project might have on InTech would need to be documented.

DeBoer concluded that simply completing this documentation and getting the project launched could easily take two to three months or more. The team needed an alternative, because according to their planning with the agency, they needed the database up and running in three months.

DeBoer recommended that rather than going through the internal corporate approval and launch processes, they should make a case to Anita McNamara, senior vice president of sales and marketing, for outsourcing this database to a service bureau or lettershop. The group agreed; expediency was their focus. An outsourced solution would also reduce the potential battles that would otherwise ensue in working with IT.

The presentation to McNamara went well, and she agreed with their assessment and their request. With twenty years of experience, including her previous post, which involved heavy direct mail spending, she was able to help the group by identifying a potential database vendor. Fast Mailing Services was a lettershop that she had used extensively for data processing, and she knew that they had some, albeit limited, database maintenance capabilities.

DeBoer, serving as the new customer database system lead, held a two-hour meeting with Fast Mailing's sales representatives, Apollo account representatives, and InTech's internal marketing team. In this meeting, they provided an overview of what they were trying to accomplish—the short-term targeted programs and the potential for additional targeted efforts in the future. The sales executives from Fast Mailing asked good questions and seemed to understand completely what InTech needed. They turned around a proposal within three days and were readily awarded the business.

Fast Mailing assigned a team of three as InTech's primary

project leaders. Everything that they proposed and then pursued was in the context of a three-month database development effort. They moved very quickly through the following steps.

Step 1: Identification of Data Sources. Unfortunately, things got off to a rough start. Some preliminary work by DeBoer and two marketing analysts suggested that there were more than fourteen different internal sources of customer data. They ranged from customer service call logs, to the sales automation tool that kept information on major accounts, to all of the different billing systems that were currently dispersed by geography and product family. While an internal enterprise resource planning (ERP) initiative was under development, it was likely twelve to eighteen months before these billing files would be consolidated.

Fast Mailing counseled DeBoer to request complete extracts from all of these systems; expecting that some of them would never be delivered. These requests were positioned as "for marketing analysis purposes" with InTech's IT group. McNamara backed DeBoer's requests with an e-mail to Craig Kenworth, head of IT, emphasizing the importance of getting this data within the two-week time frame that was placed on the request.

The data request was met with considerable disbelief by IT, since DeBoer's requests cumulatively represented more than six weeks of processing work to produce. Amidst the ERP implementation and the development of an enterprise data warehouse, IT could not dedicate human resources or system resources to meeting marketing's seemingly naïve request.

Step 2: System Design. During the first few weeks, Fast Mailing also held a series of system design meetings with InTech to work through key system development decisions. These meetings, poorly attended by the busy InTech marketing team, led to the following conclusions:

1. Separate databases should be created for each country.
2. Separate databases should be created for current customers versus prospects, since the information on these records would be different.

3. Monthly processes should be developed to move new customers from the prospect base to the appropriate customer base.

4. There will be sixteen system users at InTech; fourteen system users at the agency.

5. The database should be updated monthly so that they could report on the results of their initial programs.

6. Customers should be "householded"—that is, individuals should be brought together if they belong to the same household. Similarly, individuals should be brought together if they belong to the same business.

7. There may be multiple addresses for some of the individuals on the database. Optimally, InTech would gather and maintain both home and business addresses, since their products may appeal to individuals at home or at their place of business.

8. Other data maintained on customers should include:

   - E-mail addresses for e-mail campaigns
   - The products/services that customers have purchased, and their monthly spending on those products/services
   - Data on when InTech marketed to them and how
   - Demographics (e.g., estimated age and income, gender, household size), which Fast Mailing was able to provide through a third-party source

Fast Mailing documented all of these design issues and proceeded to design the system structure while awaiting the data. Two months into this effort, it became apparent that the data was not going to arrive. DeBoer's calls and e-mails to his contacts in IT went unanswered. DeBoer was forced to escalate this situation to McNamara. She met with Kenworth and a few of his key IT representatives, who explained their backlog situation and also questioned the validity and business importance of DeBoer's request. McNamara did all she could do to contain herself; she had to settle for IT pulling a single extract from only the U.S. billing system in the next two weeks. While less than optimal, she explained the situation to the marketing team and to Fast Mailing, and they had to proceed. The data arrived at Fast on schedule. Fast Mailing was simply overwhelmed, since the file contained all of the call detail and related billing detail from all of InTech's U.S. long-distance customers since 1996. In order for this information to be useful, Fast would have to send the data out to be processed and summarized by a much larger data processing firm. The expense for this processing equated to more than twice Fast's bid on the entire database project.

DeBoer had to unfortunately call a meeting with the broader marketing team, including their extended team of agency execs, to discuss the situation and determine next steps. They had just two weeks before the direct mail campaign for NeverDown and six weeks before the telemarketing, direct mail, and e-mail campaigns for BizPack. All of the various renditions of creative components had been printed and were ready for insertion. A telemarketing provider had been hired and trained on InTech's products. An e-mail provider was working on automating the scripts and waiting for a consolidated customer list from the database.

Very difficult decisions had to be made at this meeting. There were no good answers. The team largely blamed InTech's IT group for running interference with the effort. From this meeting, they concluded that:

- They had to continue with the targeted marketing plans, with or without the customer database.
- They would have to mail, telemarket, and e-mail to rented lists and use the assumption that 20 percent of the individuals on these lists were actually InTech's customers. From a recent market share study, they were fairly comfortable with this percentage.
- The versions of creative targeted to "customers only" would need to be scrapped. Those components would be boxed and remain in storage at the lettershop for future use.

The planning and development continued. These modifications led to six-week delays in both programs, but they were still able to implement. McNamara was pleased with the ingenuity of her team. The team was pleased with the flexibility of the agency. The agency was pleased by Fast Mailing's ability to schedule additional lettershop time and also to modify all processes to accommodate these changes. Yet the programs were dismal failures. Response rates—projected at 2 percent for mail, 3 percent for telemarketing, and 0.4 percent for e-mail—were closer to 0.12 percent, 0.18 percent, and 0.02 percent respectively.

Conclusions

Dismayed, McNamara pulled together the full project team that included Apollo, Fast Mailing, and her internal staff. Some of the agency and marketing experts concluded that direct mail, and targeted media in general, just did not work for InTech's products or InTech's markets. McNamara, and also the Fast Mailing representatives, argued that all of the compromises that were made in the planning process sacrificed any promise of successful results. The team agreed that there definitely were compromises made, and they hindered results. They also agreed that:

- They could not implement any more targeted marketing efforts unless they had a consolidated customer database. Prospect lists did not provide enough targeting to justify the expense.

- This database was a much larger project than originally scoped by InTech or by Fast Mailing. It would likely take twelve to eighteen months to fully develop, and cost several times the original estimate.

- Their programs alone could not justify this technology effort or the attendant expense. What if the programs still didn't work? Even if they did work, would they cover the expense of all of the system development work that had to be done?

InTech decided to put the pursuit of targeted marketing on hold for the remainder of the fiscal year. The company had too many other major initiatives that required time and attention. The team decided to approach IT on the matter once it had completed the ERP initiative.

InTech continued with its general advertising efforts for all products and services, across all markets, for the next fourteen months. Then, one day, McNamara was approached by Craig Kenworth. The IT group was in the process of planning phase three of its corporate warehouse, which called for the integration of a marketing data mart and related customer data entities. DeBoer and a few others from the marketing team were excited. They recognized that this was their opportunity to resurrect their customer database documentation. DeBoer became part of the planning team and served as the spokesperson for marketing's requirements in the joint application development (JAD) sessions that were part of this process.

Thirteen months later, InTech's marketing group had the marketing database capabilities that they had planned so long ago. During this time, McNamara had also begun to educate her team on the principles of targeted marketing. They had hired an agency with direct marketing expertise. They had also allocated targeted media in their annual planning process. They were now in a much better position to implement successful targeted programs.

Lessons Learned

InTech appears to be faced with enormous opportunities—opportunities to make major improvements in more targeted marketing efforts. We can learn the following from this company's short-term failures:

- Never underestimate the complexity of the technologies or processes supporting CRM.
- If CRM is new to your organization, take the time to get it right, because it may be the only chance you have to prove its value.

InTech's marketing group was given a second chance to succeed with data-driven marketing, and they did just that. Their costly mistakes can serve as valuable lessons to drive others' success.

CHAPTER FIFTEEN

CASE STUDY: BLUEWATER TECHNOLOGY GROUP

Situation Overview

Bluewater Technology Group Incorporated (BTG) is an emerging player in the world of information technology (IT) and systems consulting and integration. Its market is broad, as BTG sells its services to small, midsize, and large businesses in all vertical industries worldwide. BTG's competitors are equally broad, ranging from some of the very large firms that provide integration work to very small firms that handle network and systems administration issues. BTG is divided geographically into nine regions around the world. Within each region, the company is organized into four practice areas, with practices equating to BTG's various service offerings.

BTG's sales and marketing organization is divided primarily into these practice groups, with a vice president of sales and marketing in place for each of the four practices. Each VP has a sizable corporate staff, as well as regional sales and marketing managers within each of the nine regions, and depending on the size of the region, a staff of two to twenty under each regional manager.

As an emerging player in an already crowded yet lucrative field, BTG has an annual sales and marketing budget of more than $100 million, which has historically been divided among the practice areas based on a number of factors, including size and competitive spending patterns. Two-thirds of each practice's budget is spent on corporate efforts across all regions, with the remaining one-third spent by the regions. How budgets are spent has varied by practice area. The media spending percentages shown in Figure 15-1 were collected over the past two years. As you will notice:

- All four practices spent heavily on direct mail. Direct mail was their formula for success to date because their IT niche within the business-to-business market could most readily be reached using targeted media. In the future, they were hoping to increasingly shift that activity to electronic media, including e-mail and web-based communications.

- None of the marketing dollars was spent on general image/awareness efforts, or on corporatewide advertising or marketing promotions. The entire marketing budget went to the practice areas.

While there was a corporate requirement that all marketing efforts make mention of the broader range of BTG's services, this was often sacrificed in an effort to keep ads clean and to communicate a buttoned-up image.

Figure 15-1. BTG media expenditures.

Service Area \ Media	Direct Mail	Print Advertising in Trade Publications	Broadcast	Electronic Marketing	Conferences, Exhibits/Event Sponsorships
Integration Practice	47%	31%	7%	4%	11%
Network/Systems Administration Practice	55%	23%	9%	3%	10%
Programming Practice	36%	32%	12%	5%	15%
Software Development Practice	37%	42%	11%	4%	6%

In terms of the target market for these marketing messages, BTG recently retained a firm to conduct a formal market analysis. One of the key findings is shown in Figure 15-2, which indicates the overlap in markets for BTG's various areas of service. For example, three-fourths of those who purchase outside integration services also purchase outside network/systems administration services. More than 90 percent of those that purchase outside programming services also outsource some amount of software development. While this study did not address customers' relative spending between these service categories, or how this purchase behavior may be divided between BTG and its key competitors, it did demonstrate significant cross-purchase behavior and opportunities for BTG. The sales and marketing VPs for the various practice areas dismissed this research, which had been commissioned by the COO. The VPs maintained that:

- Their audience was very different from that of the other groups.
- Their audience recognized and appreciated the differences in BTG's practice areas, and therefore was most accustomed to hearing from practice areas rather than BTG as a whole. This justified the different creative approaches and offers driven by the four groups.

Figure 15-2. BTG cross-purchase study.

Bought → / Also Buy ↓	Integration	Network / Systems Administration	Programming	Software Development
Integration	100%	74%	71%	89%
Network/ Systems Administration	74%	100%	63%	78%
Programming	71%	63%	100%	92%
Software Development	89%	78%	92%	100%

In terms of targeting their direct market efforts, all of the practice areas could pull customer lists from their central client management system. Very little information was available on these customers for selection purposes. Oftentimes, the only targeting was by regional area.

Most of BTG's marketing efforts, however, were targeted to rented lists of IT professionals. These lists ranged from compiled Dun & Bradstreet files to subscription and technology product purchase files. Most of BTG's estimated 300 mailings per year involved the rental of several lists. As you can imagine, the practice areas within BTG were often using the same lists—sometimes within the same week!

Everyone within BTG realized that there were inefficiencies within this marketing process. But due to the size of the average sale, they maintained that this excess really had no impact on the bottom line. The catalyst for change actually came from the place least expected within BTG—from the very top.

Bob Jennings, CEO, had built the firm on this decentralized, entrepreneurial practice model. Jennings's background was in sales, and he recognized the power of empowering practice areas to operate fairly autonomously. Any internal noise raised about the inefficiencies in sales and marketing typically fell on deaf ears. He did, however, listen to his customers. Jennings happened to be golfing with Cary Martinez, the CIO of Martinez Metalworking, one of BTG's longest-standing clients. Martinez lightheartedly joked with Jennings about the deluge of mail that he receives from BTG. "Sometimes an entire inbox of colorful BTG clutter . . . " was his comment.

That comment stuck with Jennings, all the way back to the office the next day. Jennings called a special meeting with the four sales and marketing VPs to discuss the matter. That meeting proved frustrating, because no one could provide specifics regarding their sales and marketing activities. They could only hypothesize about what any customer would be receiving from BTG as a whole. The meeting ended with Jennings's firm reprimand to the VPs: "Our customers are getting too much irrelevant information from us; it's up to you to fix it!"

CRM Implementation

The four sales and marketing VPs had to move into immediate action. This task was going to be easier said than done because:

- Plans, budgets, and schedules were already established six months in advance. Agencies were busy developing creative.
- They had done little tracking historically of what worked and what didn't work. They did not know and could not determine which programs, if any, should be cut.
- A good portion of the budget and related activity was in the hands of the regional sales and marketing managers. These disparate efforts were also several months into development.

While all of these factors were fairly imposing, they knew that they had to push forward with this initiative. When Jennings said that he wanted something, he wanted it fast. The VPs went into a three-day planning session and began to identify how their sales and marketing initiatives could be improved. The ideas discussed ranged from very broad, long-term strategic initiatives to some very tactical immediate improvements. Susan Cann, head of the integration practice area and perhaps the most sophisticated in her CRM thinking, summarized and categorized these ideas as follows:

Technology
- We need to consolidate our client and prospect files so that we know who all of the contacts are within a company.
- We need to maintain key information on all of our individual contacts, including their titles and job functions, and the SIC codes and sizes of the sites with which they are associated.
- We need a way to continually update valuable information on our clients and new contacts that we meet at client sites and multiple locations, as well as develop an understanding of their future anticipated needs.
- We need to keep track of what we e-mail and direct mail to our clients and to our prospects; we need to keep promotion history on a client marketing database.

- We need a user-friendly means of accessing all of this data so that key individuals within each of our practice areas can analyze and select relevant information.
- We need to fully understand campaign management.
- We need to fully understand and know how to use data mining.
- We need a means of projecting customers' lifetime value and what the future revenue and profitability of each of our clients might be.

Planning and Budgeting

- We need to work together on our marketing plans, to make sure that our major campaigns do not directly overlap or conflict with each other.
- We need to begin to plan and budget our efforts so that we have built-in flexibility. If programs do not work, we certainly should not repeat them.
- Planning and particularly budgeting should somehow be handled consistently across the groups. Currently, we each take a different approach.
- Budgets should somehow be based on anticipated return on investment (ROI) of each campaign.

Programs and Packages

- We need to somehow look at the BTG brand across our business units and across our campaigns. Currently, we seem to have four distinct brands.
- All promotional materials need a common look and feel.
- We need to begin to base media and creative decisions on campaign objectives (e.g., lead generation versus sale) and potential return.
- We need to test offers.
- We need to do customer or market segmentation and modeling to improve results.

- Results of all programs should be consolidated and shared, so we know what works and what doesn't work across practice areas. Today we are redundantly testing.

The VPs felt good about this list and believed they had leveraged much of what they had been reading in CRM trade publications and books and also hearing at conferences. At the same time, they were somewhat overwhelmed because this list of initiatives was daunting. Jennings was looking for a quick fix and seldom entertained longer-term initiatives driven by sales and marketing. Yet they knew that some of the longer-term initiatives were absolutely essential in order to drive tactical improvements.

Their follow-up meeting with Jennings was just around the corner. They developed a presentation to gain approval for moving forward on all of the initiatives itemized. They were actually quite proud of their out-of-the-box, strategic thinking. However, surmising that Jennings was actually expecting them to have the problem fixed when they met, they had to keep the presentation as brief as possible. They hurriedly created a presentation deck that outlined all of the projects as next steps. They did not think that the CEO would approve all of the projects on the list, but decided to list them all in hopes that at least some of them would strike a chord and gain his approval.

Cassandra Jones, the most senior of the four VPs, presented. Jennings unfortunately seemed somewhat distracted throughout the meeting and asked few questions. The bright side, however, was that he understood that it could take a little longer to fix the problem at hand.

The team received the results they expected. Jennings did not approve all of the projects, but did give the go-ahead on the following two initiatives:

- *A Common "Look and Feel" for All Marketing Efforts.* Agency guidelines would be created around use of the company logo, colors, and other general standards.
- *Segmentation and Modeling to Improve Results.* Susan Cann

knew that Jennings did not really understand what this directive meant, but he liked the idea of improving results.

The team met in the late afternoon, after their meeting with the CEO. They were now puzzled about their next steps and questioned:

- Did Jennings really understand the importance of all of these initiatives?
- As a technology company, the VPs thought the CEO would select at least one technology initiative, yet he did not. Did he understand the importance of having the right data in order to do segmentation or modeling?
- Wouldn't they need to somehow bring the practice areas together for planning—beyond planning the common look and feel—in order to significantly impact what clients and prospects are receiving?

The team of VPs knew that the approved projects would not even come close to solving their contact strategy challenges. They could not pursue any modeling or segmentation without consolidated, meaningful customer data. The "common look and feel" initiative would only make their problem of overmarketing more noticeable to customers.

At this point, they decided that their best course of action would be to halfheartedly pursue the "common look and feel initiative," because these results would be visible to Jennings, and to let the modeling and segmentation concept, as well as the rest of their good ideas and intentions, be delayed indefinitely.

Conclusions

Looking back at this attempt to bring customer-centric marketing to their organization, the VPs arrived at the following conclusions:

- BTG as an organization needs significant education on the concepts, constructs, and value of data-driven marketing.

Senior management, as well as the line workers, need to begin to understand how other companies use data-driven marketing, marketing databases, and analyses such as lifetime value and measurement to drive bottom-line results. The primary job of the VPs, then, should be to educate before they implement.

- The VPs should have prioritized their list of "good ideas" and identified the dependencies in their meeting with the CEO. They should have presented a logical, phased approach rather than just a list of what could be done.

- They should have emphasized the importance of the infrastructure as a critical factor for improvements in results.

- They should have built a gradual business case, projecting cost savings as well as incremental revenues, from data-driven investments.

The VPs learned valuable lessons in this initial attempt to craft a data-driven marketing plan for the company. They resolved to work on the general awareness and education of the company over the coming six months. They decided to develop an internal communications electronic newsletter that would be distributed across the company. This newsletter would contain case studies and short articles designed to get the broader organization thinking about data-driving marketing and broader CRM issues.

Lessons Learned

There appear to be major opportunities for increasing sales and marketing efficiencies within BTG, as within many organizations. However, these efforts:

- Typically involve a variety of business process and infrastructure dependencies, most of which are not readily visible.

- Frequently involve broader organizational development and change.

- Always involve educating all levels of the organization—particularly key stakeholders—on the merits of CRM.

These lessons are keys to any organization's CRM success.

CHAPTER SIXTEEN

CASE STUDY: PARTNERS INSURANCE COMPANY

Situation Overview

Partners Insurance Company was formed in 1919, when the founders raised $1 million to launch the National Safe Partners Insurance Company. The new company insured returning World War I service personnel against disabilities caused by wartime accidents and illness. National Safe Partners was an early provider of what is now known as multiline insurance, in that it also provided auto and life insurance. By 1923, the company established a charter as Partners Charter Insurance Company, selling insurance to the populace at large.

By the early 1990s, Partners had firmly established itself as a leading provider of automobile and home protection insurance, ranking number four in the United States in terms of annual revenue. However, the life insurance business was not measuring up to the same lofty standards, ranking twenty-fifth in the country.

One of the reasons for this disparity could be traced to their captive agents' compensation policy. Agents were paid a much lower commission for selling life insurance than standard property and automobile insurance. In addition, life insurance was a much more complex product, with various features related to investment potential. It was also a harder "sell." Most prospective customers understood the need to insure their car or house, but it was much more difficult a proposition to sell a customer on the need to insure against one's own mortality. In an attempt to expand alternative nonagent-based distribution methods, Partners Insurance established the Direct Response Unit (DRU) in 1992. DRU had its own organizational structure, with a vice president reporting to the president of the Partners Life Insurance Division. Five directors within DRU led five departments: financial, information systems, marketing, actuarial, and customer service.

Initial Challenges

Three immediate challenges faced the new DRU: product development, target market identification, and the integration of this direct response business into the agent-dominated culture.

Product Development

The company wanted to ensure that any products offered through alternative channels posed no significant threat to the agents' revenue stream. There was also an early recognition that more complex life insurance products containing investment components, such as universal or whole life, were difficult to sell without agent intervention. Therefore, the first products developed for sale by the DRU were accidental death (AD) and accidental death and dismemberment (AD&D).

The DRU also pursued new product development. The focus of its efforts was mainly on creating products that would not compete with the core line of agency life products. One of the early innovations was the development of "trial" coverage, which was offered to insurance prospects at no charge for a limited ninety-day period. After the trial period, the coverage would be billed at standard rates. The advantage of this offer was the opportunity for

Partners to get "a foot in the door" by offering free insurance coverage, albeit for a very limited period. The disadvantage was not surprising; many customers canceled their insurance coverage after the trial period.

Target Market Identification

When first incorporated as a separate corporate entity, the DRU concentrated its marketing efforts on current corporate, agent-sold customers. However, these sales efforts were not very successful due to the fact that the agent-based customers were not necessarily in need of supplemental life products. Partners found it much more profitable to form alliances with banks and retail stores with captive credit card customers. In exchange for a specified compensation mainly based on sales, the company gained access to its partners' customer lists. Another advantage of partnering with credit card issuers was the fact that Partners could implement the billing of the insurance via the cooperating company's credit card operations.

Traditional Agent Focus

Because the new unit was established from the product and agent point of view, the emphasis was, "How do we make money and not upset the apple cart?" The emphasis unfortunately was not on customer needs.

Marketing Overview

The DRU's marketing programs were largely untargeted. While it now had access to several captive lists, its promotional approach was to essentially send third-class promotional mailings to everyone on the list as often as possible. These mailings were product- and benefit-focused and did not vary by customer segment. In fact, current customers were being solicited for products that they already had purchased.

CRM Implementation

The DRU realized that it was lacking and in desperate need of customer intelligence. Senior management identified a few key initiatives that were vital to the ongoing viability as a business. These included:

- Opening job requisitions and, over the course of a year, hiring a team of eight outside resources, all with significant insurance marketing experience.
- Approving funding and resources for the development of a marketing database to initially support the DRU's needs, but over time to scale to support Partners' broader CRM needs. This database was outsourced, and the initial implementation of the system was up and running six months after the contract was signed.
- Modifying business plans and budgets to reflect a more aggressive level of investment and related return over the next year.

The related business goals of these initiatives were as follows:

1. Increase average annual premium per household by 2.5 percent.
2. Reduce cost per sale by 3 percent.
3. Increase cross-selling and upselling to current customer base by 2 percent.

Once the new staff was in place and the database was up and running, Partners found that it was able to begin looking at its customer and prospect base on both a household and an individual level.

Customer Lifetime Value

Since Partners was now able to consolidate financial information by individual and household across various product lines, it was finally able to estimate a customers' lifetime value (LTV)—both the customers' contribution to date and an estimate of future potential. The components that had a positive contribution on LTV were premium paid over lifetime and also estimated value of referrals to other lines of business. The three components that deducted from an individual's LTV were solicitation expense, fulfillment expense, and claims. By aggregating this information by product, projected LTV could be estimated for each new customer, for each product line.

Once the DRU had developed projected customer-level and product-level LTV, it was challenged to substantially change the way that it planned and executed marketing efforts. By combining the product-level financial information with individual-level projected probability of response and payment, the list selection process was driven by anticipated individual customer profitability.

Segment Focus

Another early initiative was to perform segmentation analysis on nonbuyers. It became clear that the current set of product offerings wasn't meeting the needs of a core group of potential customers. This information, combined with primary and secondary research, led the DRU to develop insurance products and offers to meet needs of specific customer segments. Cancer surgical insurance products were among those developed as part of this initiative.

The company was slowly warming up to the customer-centric business approach. The DRU reorganized into two divisions: New Customer Acquisition and Policy-Owner Marketing.

Customer Service Challenges

Partners faced a dichotomy in terms of its technology and systems. As described, the relatively new marketing database handled the proactive aspects of customer communications. However, the customer service system was relatively unchanged since its inception back in 1982 and was operating completely independently of the marketing database and other systems. No data, process, or functionality had been established to assist the customer service area in differentiating callers.

Partners employed an internal inbound call center staffed, twenty-four hours a day, seven days a week. Individuals calling to cancel their insurance policy generated approximately 70 percent of the call volume. As standard operating procedure, customer service representatives were instructed to process cancellation requests as quickly and politely as possible and to attempt to capture the reason for cancellation for tracking purposes. Compensation of the customer service representatives was based on their adherence to these simple standards.

Customer Service Opportunity and Success

Partners realized its weakness, but with no bottom-line rationale it was difficult to change the call center from one of expedience to one of service. The company had to start small. It selected fifteen high-performing, personable customer service representatives to participate. The representatives were provided a three-week intensive training course on customer retention strategies. They were instructed to try to retain every customer that called over the course of the next two months. Relatedly, each customer that was "saved" was to receive a personalized thank-you letter directly from the service representative.

The DRU found that it required an average of eight minutes to attempt to retain a customer that called in to cancel. This was far more than the overall average of 1.5 minutes per call. It became evident that the numbers had to be carefully scrutinized on this new initiative.

Partners then developed individual-level calculations that projected the additional premium that would result if a customer were retained. Once it was determined that inbound customer service termination calls could be differentiated by product, the next logical step was to determine which other variables could be utilized to treat customers on a one-to-one basis. First, duration of product ownership was considered. It was discovered that while it was not cost-justifiable to attempt to retain all customers who owned a particular product, it was profitable to attempt to "save" customers who had owned the product for a more extended period. This was especially true of customers who owned trial coverage products. Therefore, the process was refined to incorporate a combination of product ownership and duration.

Next, customer characteristics (e.g., purchase behaviors, media and channel preferences, demographic and geographic characteristics) were included in the differentiation process. Since several variables were now at work, the customer service reps needed an automated indicator to let them know whether they should attempt to retain a particular inbound cancellation call. The data mining functionality within the marketing database was employed to make that determination based on demographic and behavioral information. On a weekly basis, the new "save" indicator along with the necessary customer identification information was fed from the marketing database to the call center system. The program—while operationally costly—was a big success. It resulted in an estimated $3.7 million in annual premiums from "saved" customers within the first year.

Conclusions

The DRU's CRM initiatives continued to evolve over a four-year period. During that time:

- The company continued to hire talent, as well as train existing resources on the principles of direct marketing.
- The company's systems became increasingly sophisticated to support business needs and applications.
- The breadth of products grew, as it became apparent to Partners that the Direct Response Unit could generate million of dollars of extremely profitable business.

In 2001, Partners completely abandoned its captive agent channel, and direct marketing—via the Web, direct mail, and call centers— became the sole focus of the business.

Lessons Learned

Partners at DRU learned several valuable lessons through these initial CRM initiatives:

1. Building the infrastructure—the resources, systems, and processes—can be time-consuming and costly. However, it provides the necessary foundation for any CRM strategic initiatives.

2. Competing channels and conflicting goals and objectives can endanger CRM initiatives.

3. Though difficult, it can be a very worthy endeavor to apply CRM principles within an operational environment.

SYSTEMS AND TECHNOLOGY TO SUPPORT CRM

This appendix explains some of the more common customer relationship management (CRM) systems and applications in today's marketplace. It is not intended to serve as a definitive or comprehensive guide to all of the many systems alternatives available, but rather provides a broad overview of many of the essential CRM systems offerings.

Customer Database

Crucial to almost all CRM systems is a central, consolidated collection of customer data. This may be termed a data warehouse, data mart, data store, or database, depending on the level of detail contained and the primary purpose of the system. This collection of customer data typically supports several primary business applications ranging from data-driven marketing to customer service. The data and processing involved in a customer database can be extremely complex; on the other hand, the capability of the database itself is typically limited. It relies on online transaction processing (OLTP) systems to collect and process data, and it also feeds data to OLTP applications.

Think of a customer database as a storehouse for data that is created or collected by other systems. A defining feature of a customer database is that it is customer-centric; customer data is the central focus of the system. Great effort is devoted to gathering, consolidating, and then maintaining data related to customers. This data may include:

- *Customer Contact Information*: name, address, e-mail, phone, business information
- *Profile Information*: demographics such as age and estimated income on consumers; firmographics such as SIC code and company size or businesses
- *Purchase History*: purchase date, source, product category, specific items, amount, channel, payment method
- *Promotion History*: promotion date, source code, offer, package
- *Other Interactions*: customer service calls, website visits
- *Derived Data*: data related to customers, such as behavioral summaries, segment codes, lifetime value calculations, and model scores

You can begin to imagine the wide range of opportunities for using this data for purposes ranging from market sizing and mapping applications, to analysis of customer purchase patterns and trends, to selection of target markets for sales or marketing programs.

Before this data enters the customer base—that is, before this data can be used for any business applications—it typically requires significant cleansing, consolidation, and transformation. Just a few of the most important processing routines include:

- *Address Standardization*. Applying standards to postal addresses ensures deliverability and also enhances the overall quality of your data.

- *Merge/Purge and Consolidation.* Identification of duplicate records and corresponding transactions is critical to gaining a complete understanding of customer characteristics and behaviors.

- *Data Transformation.* Detailed transactional data is often not useful because of its granularity, diverse formats, or cumulative volume. Simple transformations could involve associating activities with regions. A more complex transformation may involve linking behaviors with marketing programs.

These and many other processes ensure that your customer data—although it can never be completely accurate—is as clean and useful as possible before it enters the customer base.

Decision Support

Most customer databases directly or indirectly further one or multiple decision support systems (DSS). Most CRM-related reporting and analysis is multidimensional in nature, often requiring access to granular-level customer detail. Users are typically looking at several key dimensions, probing with questions such as:

- How many customers purchased a specific product (or from a product category) last year, but not this year?
- Which products are most frequently purchased by new customers? Are these products also most frequently purchased by our best customers?
- How many customer service calls in January are generated by new subscribers?

The questions users may pose and their related data needs are endless.

There are many different categories of query and reporting tools to support a wide range of users and their related DSS needs. Many of these tools allow nontechnical users to construct their analyses without having an understanding of the underlying technical structure of the database. In practice, it is not uncommon to have a suite of tools to support the decision-making requirements of various users throughout the organization. Some will need very basic reporting functions and features; others will need very powerful, complex online analytical processing (OLAP) or relational online analytical processing (ROLAP) capabilities.

Marketing Automation

In organizations with a significant marketing function, campaign development and management is a key CRM application. Granular customer data is particularly helpful in the development of direct mail, telemarketing, and e-mail campaigns. The marketing department's needs may be met by a campaign management tool that is integrated with the customer database; alternatively, the marketing organization may take a subset of the customer data and develop a stand-alone marketing database or specialized data mart. The use of campaign management tools is becoming increasingly commonplace as the technology continues to evolve.

The functionality of a campaign management tool is very different from that of any other application. Marketers have become extremely sophisticated in terms of their selection of lists for mailings, telemarketing, and e-mail campaigns. A direct marketing effort, for example, often entails:

- Testing various offers and creative packages across subsets of the selected universe
- Varying timing, sequence, media, and other factors
- Measuring response, revenue, and return on investment by offer, timing, media, creative, and customer segment

This data and functionality is used to generate, track, and measure marketing promotions. The essentials in a campaign management environment are the ability to:

- Track the overall results of any marketing promotion, in terms of response, revenue relative to cost, and other measures.

- Identify specifically who responded and the characteristics of those responders.
- Identify the cumulative impact of multiple marketing promotions and other customer interactions on response.

Data Mining

Data mining is increasingly used as a generic term to describe analytical procedures that derive meaningful findings from data. As a result, those involved in various aspects of CRM may use this term to refer to an OLAP tool while others may view data mining as those applications that resemble artificial intelligence. For our purposes, we use the term *data mining* to refer to tools and techniques designed to identify and explore complex relationships that are not otherwise apparent through intuitive analysis.

Data mining uses complex algorithms and statistical techniques to examine multidimensional relationships and identify patterns, relationships, and trends. The primary difference between data mining and decision support tools is that with decision support tools, users start with a hypothesis they are trying to prove. Data mining, on the other hand, begins with an examination of the wealth of data that is available and allows the patterns to emerge.

Thus, data mining applications typically use the most granular detail from a customer database. Clean, standardized data is critical to most of these applications because they are often 100 percent dependent on this data at its face value to generate results. It is difficult to see patterns in data clouded by lax standards

One of the key functions of a CRM data mining capability is integration with the campaign management process. The ideal environment would allow the user to readily transition from the discovery of a target audience definition in a mining environment to target audience selection, offer selection, and fulfillment.

Sales Force Automation

Sales force automation (SFA) tools are primarily focused on supporting the data needs of a direct sales force. These software applications allow salespeople to track their ongoing communications and relationships with their accounts.

In terms of data, an SFA application typically contains a subset of the most relevant information from the customer database, in addition to:

- *Detailed Contact Information*: the name of a senior executive's assistant or each contact's role in the decision-making process
- *Detailed Interaction History*: the history of direct contacts—calls, visits, contract negotiations, key drivers—with the customer or prospect and any next steps
- *Rankings or Scores*: any system that the salesperson uses to grade the size and relative importance of the relationship

This data may be consolidated within the customer database or another central repository in order to analyze sales performance and size future business opportunities. In addition to this synchronization, the functionality of an SFA application typically includes:

- *Analysis.* Typically the application searches on a wide range of fields in order to narrow down the universe to a small collection of contacts.
- *Reporting.* This function includes reporting on overall activity, the salesperson's book of business, budgets, and forecasts.
- *Productivity Features.* SFA systems are designed around making the mobile sales force as productive as possible. Consequently, productivity functions are made available to the salesperson such as automated tickler systems, calendar management, customized word processing applications, scripting, call list management, and order processing.
- *Sales Pipeline Forecasting.* Summarizing and sizing future sales opportunities may be based on anticipated time, dollar amounts, and other criteria.

Customer Care

Customer care applications cover a broad spectrum of systems including call centers, customer service centers, help desks, and reservation applications. These "frontline systems" are designed to support representatives who have direct one-to-one interaction with customers or prospective customers. They are designed to provide representatives with the most relevant information on which to take immediate action.

In terms of data, these systems typically contain a subset of the name and address information that is in a customer database and, depending on the specific application, may also include a subset of granular transaction detail and other customer activity.

These systems are often linked to other operational systems such as inventory management, fulfillment, and accounts receivable. In addition to providing access to relevant information, these systems often process transactions. This typically involves:

- Customer identification
- Transaction capture and/or location
- Call scripting, including accessing relevant product and promotion information, as well as potentially trigger-based upselling/cross-selling strategies and scripts

Interactive, Online Solutions

These solutions are still in their infancy and currently represent a collection of diverse applications, ranging from web customization tools to outbound e-mail engines. Many vendors currently offer solutions for specific online applications. The current challenge is that most of these systems are not integrated with any other customer information–based systems. They tend to create and maintain silo databases of e-mail addresses, click stream activity, and/or potentially other information.

A sizable challenge to integrating these systems with centralized customer database is the data. Most customer databases today still lack accurate e-mail addresses for a majority of customers. On the other hand, most e-marketing systems (e.g., e-mail databases and web tools) do not maintain accurate customer name and address information. Therefore, integrating these disparate data sources often proves futile, since linking the files is not possible.

Nonetheless, it is critical to bring the data in these systems together. Some of these data-dependent, related online applications include:

- *Personalization.* Broadly speaking, personalization encompasses the presentation of relevant messages, products, and targeted promotions to each web visitor.
- *Ad Targeting.* This application is a form of personalization that relies heavily on previous ad click behavior to drive future ad banners.
- *E-Mail Campaign Management.* A subset of the broader campaign management category noted previously, tools specifically designed to generate e-mail campaigns usually have a heavy emphasis on website links and subsequent tracking of click behavior.
- *Collaborative Filtering.* The process of using individual clickstream data, purchase history, explicit preferences, and product similarities to drive personalization recommendations.

CRM Opportunities

Increased Revenues

1. Maximize the value of existing customers by:
   — Improving cross-sell
   — Improving upsell
   — Increasing margins
   — Enhancing activation/product usage
   — Enhancing reactivation
   — Increasing retention
   — Practicing selective nonretention
   — Reducing cost-to-service

2. Enhance customer acquisition by:
   — Improving selective/targeted acquisition
   — Increasing value of new customers
   — Increasing number of new profitable customers

— Increasing retention of new customers
— Increasing market penetration
— Controlling growth

Improved Efficiencies/Reduced Expenses

1. Realize sales efficiencies by:
   — Increasing sales force productivity
   — Reducing cost per sale
   — Reducing expense per salesperson
   — Increasing penetration on key accounts
   — Improving conversion rates
   — Increasing sales in targeted segments
   — Reducing cost per contact
   — Improving efficiency of lead generation and management
   — Improving ability to measure sales force performance

2. Realize service efficiencies by:
   — Improving conversation or close rates
   — Improving service call completion and resolution rates
   — Reducing service expenses per customer
   — Improving ability to measure service representative performance
   — Improving customer responsiveness

3. Archive marketing efficiencies by:
   — Improving response rates
   — Reducing marketing costs per contact/response
   — Eliminating duplicates or unmailable addresses
   — Reducing misdirected messages
   — Improving media selection, placement, and positioning for advertising efforts
   — Improving abilities to measure performance of marketing efforts

4. Recognize operational efficiencies by:
   — Improving access to/and sharing customer information
   — Reducing redundant and/or wasted effort
   — Increasing integration of key business processes
   — Decreasing fulfillment costs
   — Reducing system and data maintenance costs
   — Improving data quality
   — Reducing fraud
   — Reducing cancellations/returns
   — Reducing inventory costs
   — Improving the ability to measure performance of key business processes

Increased Competitive Differentiation

1. Increase customer knowledge by:
   — Profiling the customer base
   — Segmenting your customer base
   — Understanding share of customer wallet
   — Estimating customer lifetime value
   — Measuring customer retention and attrition
   — Understanding customer product purchase and usage trends
   — Approximating customer loyalty
   — Monitoring customer satisfaction levels
   — Understanding product impact on customer performance
   — Understanding customer needs, attitudes, and preferences

2. Increase knowledge of market opportunities by:
   — Calculating market share
   — Analyzing market growth
   — Developing specific geographic, vertical, or lifestyle niches
   — Identifying underperforming groups
   — Identifying geographic opportunities
   — Identifying valuable market segment opportunities
   — Expanding channels

— Targeting new geographies/locations
— Identifying new product development opportunities

3. Increase knowledge of competition by:
   — Studying differences in business dynamics in competitive versus noncompetitive markets
   — Measuring customer loyalty in the face of new competition

4. Improve customer service by:
   — Delivering personalized and superior customer communication
   — Delivering personalized and superior customer service
   — Improving service quality

GLOSSARY OF TERMS

The glossary that follows provides practical definitions of some of the more frequently used CRM-related terms. You may have your own interpretations of these concepts; that's natural with any broad business movement. If not, this reference provides you with a good starting point that enables you to "talk the talk."

1:1 – one-to-one marketing
A marketing strategy that recognizes that all customers are unique. For companies to deliver maximum customer value and thereby increase customer profitability, they must meet these unique customer needs and purchase behaviors.

action plan
A general term for any business blueprint that spells out in detail the specific tasks, timing, and resource requirements necessary to meet a stated goal.

active customer
A subjective and situational designation of a customer who is engaged in a relationship with an organization; typically based on their recency of transacting business.

attrition
The typically undesirable decline in numbers of customers or specific customer groups, or a decline in their level of activity. Customer retention efforts are employed to curb attrition; customer reactivation efforts are employed to reactivate attritors.

business case
A presentation that financially justifies a proposed course of action. Typically, a business case quantifies the short- and longer-term benefits of a new initiative relative to initial and ongoing costs. A business case with positive return-on-investment parameters has a greater likelihood of approval.

business intelligence
Concise and useful information about the state of an organization, its assets (including its customers), external forces (economic, political, global) and its competitors.

business metrics
Measures of organizational performance. These typically include financial metrics related to revenues, expenses, and income, as well as metrics related to employee productivity, product and channel performance, and marketing effectiveness. Customer metrics—measures of customer acquisition, retention, and monetization—should round out most organizations' business metrics.

business model
An organization's general mode of operations or how an organization accomplishes its stated goals and acts on its vision. The method by which a company realizes revenues.

business rules

Explicit, systematic instructions that detail how an organization's processes should handle a given situation. Business rules may be as broad-reaching as overall operating procedures, or may be as contained as the automated processes to handle various types of data. Business rules are also sometimes used as an alternative to statistical methods for segmentation and list generation.

business-to-business (B2B)

Commerce that involves selling products/services to businesses, institutions, and other organizations. These business customers may consume or may resell these products/services.

business-to-consumer (B2C)

Commerce that involves selling products/services to individuals or households for personal consumption.

buzzword

A trendy term that quickly gains favor, particularly in the business community, and, almost as quickly, fades from common usage.

call center

The locations where inbound (calls coming in) and/or outbound (calls going out) phone contacts are handled for a given company. Call centers may handle sales, service, and/or support issues. Increasingly, call centers are being retooled as "customer care," "customer interaction," or "customer contact" centers that may also handle e-mail, Web, and wireless interactions, as well as traditional phone-based activity.

campaign management

A process of planning, budgeting, implementing, and measuring targeted marketing efforts.

channel

Means of product/service distribution such as retail stores, catalog, e-commerce, Internet, and direct sales.

competitive advantage

A strategic edge that one organization has over others in its market. This may be a better product, a lower price, unique channels of distribution, unique supplier relationships, or exceptional means of sales and marketing promotion. Increasingly, organizations are relying on the customer differential—the loyalty of their customers—as their unique differentiator and source of competitive advantage.

competitive intelligence

Information on the products, services, goals, strategies, plans, capabilities, and perceptions of other providers in your marketplace.

contact strategy

A plan that outlines your intended communications with an individual or group of customers or prospective customers. This plan should address the frequency of contact, the objectives of each contact, the specific timing of contacts, the channel and media format, the specific messages and offers for each contact, and the desired result of each contact. Developing a contact strategy encourages you to address ongoing interactions with a customer or group of customers.

conversion rate

The percentage of inquiries (or leads) who "take the next step" by making a purchase and becoming customers.

cost per acquired customer

The average expenditure for generating a new customer. Sales and marketing expenses and resources, as well as specific infrastructure expenses, are typically included in acquisition costs, and then allocated across the number of new customers generated in a specific period of time.

cost per inquiry (lead)

The average expenditure for generating an inquiry or lead.

cross-selling
A strategy that involves marketing products from additional categories or departments to an existing customer. An apparel retailer might cross-sell belts or shoes to purchasers of men's suits.

customer
The focus of all CRM efforts. A customer may be defined as a single individual, a household of individuals, a branch office of a company, a regional, national or global headquarters of an organization, or the most appropriate definition that suits the business needs of the company. Increasingly, organizations are viewing their employees and business partners as additional "customer" constituencies, and terms such as ERM (Employee Relationship Management) and PRM (Partner Relationship Management) have emerged in many business models.

customer acquisition
Strategies and programs designed to entice prospective customers to purchase an organization's goods and/or services. Also known as prospecting.

customer care
This term most often references customer service functions and responsibilities in an organization. Customer service is increasingly becoming a proactive, as well as reactive, practice in many organizations.

customer conversion
The process and art of "closing a sale"—converting an inquiry or lead to a customer.

customer database
One of the primary components of a customer information management solution. This is a repository of customer name and contact information, demographic, psychographic, interest/lifestyle, firmographic, or other characteristics, interaction and purchase history, and projections of future behavior and value. This system

may also be termed a customer data warehouse, customer data mart, or marketing data mart.

customer development
The process of increasing and deepening customer relationship value with targeted strategies, programs, promotions, and/or contacts designed to stimulate up-sell and cross-sell programs.

customer experience
The sum total of all interactions that a customer has with all areas and aspects of your organization, across all touchpoints. The quality of the customer's experience with an organization will likely affect their satisfaction and future purchase behavior.

Customer Experience Cycle
This encompasses all of the events that a customer goes through before, during, and after the purchase of the organization's goods or services.

customer information management
A broad term that encompasses the collection, transformation, maintenance, and ongoing management of customer information. This customer information could range from names and addresses to a history of sales and marketing contacts to a history of purchase or service-related transactions. Increasingly, organizations are augmenting behavioral data on customers with additional information on needs, attitudes, and preferences collected through online and offline surveys.

customer intelligence
Relevant, useful information about customers. Gaining increased customer intelligence involves a combination of ongoing research as well as data collection, data analysis, and interpretation.

customer lifecycle
Encompasses the period from when a customer purchases his or her first product or service through attrition. Organizations can

analyze lifecycle patterns to identify the optimal sequencing and timing of specific product and service offerings. This information can be used to develop the overarching customer contact strategy.

customer lifetime value
An estimate of the total value of a customer over his or her tenure as a customer with an organization. The calculation is based on profits to date, and assumes increases or decreases in future profits. These profits are forecasted across the estimated tenure (lifetime) as a customer using a net present value formula.

customer loyalty
A measure of the strength, depth, and tenure of an organization's relationship with any given customer.

customer metrics
Measures of the quantity and quality of the relationships that an organization has with its customer. These metrics should relate to customer acquisition, retention, purchase and service activity, value, attrition, and reactivation.

customer migration
The movement of a customer from one distinct segment to another, typically based on changes in purchase behavior or other characteristics.

customer preferences
The needs and desires of a customer for specific product and service attributes.

customer profiling
A rigorous examination of the key behavioral, demographic, psychographic, firmographic, and/or attitudinal characteristics of a customer base. Customer profiles are typically developed for each distinct customer segment.

customer purchase cycle
The series of decision processes and events that a customer undertakes before, during, and after the procurement of a given product or service.

customer reactivation
Strategies, programs, promotions, and/or contacts designed to stimulate repurchase activity of inactive customers.

customer relationship management (CRM)
A business strategy that focuses on optimizing the value an organization delivers to customers, and, as a result, the value an organization receives from customers. This strategy requires redirecting business focus, organizational structure, business metrics, customer interaction, business practices, and technology capabilities to optimize the customer experience.

customer retention
Strategies, programs, promotions, and/or contacts designed to increase loyalty and thereby discourage customers from defecting from or otherwise abandoning their relationships with an organization.

customer satisfaction
A measure of how pleased a given customer or group of customers is with their relationship with an organization.

customer scorecard
A concise report of key customer metrics that measures the activity and overall customer value of the relationship between an organization and a given group of their customers. The scorecard represents a key business decision-making tool that can help monitor the success of CRM initiatives, and suggest new tactics and strategies for improving customer relationships.

customer touchpoints
All of the active and passive interaction points that a customer has

with an organization. These can include outbound advertising and marketing efforts, direct sales contacts, customer service interactions, fulfillment centers, return desks, site visits, public relations, and many other corporate communications and contacts.

data collection
The ongoing gathering of information about customers and their needs, interests, characteristics, and behaviors.

data hygiene
Processes focused on improving information quality. Automated processes such as address standardization, data verification, consolidation, and householding are applied to customer data to increase data consistency, accuracy, precision, and reliability.

data quality
The extent to which your data are valuable. Typical measures of data quality include accuracy (is it correct?); coverage (is it available across all customers or entities?); recency (is it current?); and precision (how exact are the values?).

data mining
The process of analyzing data to uncover trends, correlations, and other directional findings. This typically involves sophisticated computer software and statistical analysis tools designed to readily identify relevant information.

data security
Refers to the procedures and precautions taken by an organization to safeguard the customer information.

database marketing
A key component of CRM that involves targeting communications and offers to individuals based on their propensity to respond.

decision support tools
A very broad term used to describe software applications designed to generate and deliver business intelligence.

demographics
Information about an individual or group of individuals such as income, age, household size, automobile ownership, education, occupation, or other characteristics.

e-business
The ability to conduct business anytime and anywhere, with these interactions between an organization and its customers or partners being enabled by new technologies—many of which involve the Web.

firmographics
Information about a business such as industry classification, the number of employees, number of locations, and annual revenues.

household
A grouping of individuals typically within a physical address.

householding
An automated process of grouping the data on multiple individuals to a single household.

inactive customer
A subjective and situational designation of a customer who is no longer engaged in a relationship with an organization; typically based on the lack of business transactions within some anticipated period of time.

inquiry
A lead; a prospective customer who has taken an action to indicate interest or intent in purchasing your product/service.

insourcing
Managing a process or handling a function with internal resources and capabilities.

lead generation
Strategies and programs designed to prompt prospective customers to inquire or otherwise indicate interest in potentially purchasing a product/service.

lifestyle data
Information on an individual's hobbies, leisure interests, and media consumption habits and activities.

marketing automation
A broad term that refers to marketing production workflow and campaign management systems. Many believe that marketing planning and implementation is one of the most labor-intensive and least process-driven areas of an organization; thus, the interest in marketing automation technologies.

mass customization
Advancements in manufacturing and communications technology allowing for products to be tailored to individual customers or groups of customers based on their needs and preferences.

media
Means of customer communication, such as television, radio, newspapers, magazines, outdoor, direct mail, websites, and email.

meta data
"Data about data." Frequently referred to as a data dictionary that provides the definition of a data element, its source, and its field size/characteristics. Many customer information efforts fail because data are not appropriately defined, making it very difficult for business users to use the data.

modeling

Applying statistical techniques to create predictive equations around the likelihood of a given action, outcome, or occurrence. Modeling in the context of CRM generally relates to examining past customer behavior in order to predict future customer behavior.

monetization

To generate revenue from a group of customers or from a business channel.

online analytical processing (OLAP)

Systems designed to support batch-based decision support, analysis, and marketing automation needs. OLAP systems do not involve operational processes or applications.

online transaction processing (OLTP)

Systems designed to support real-time, operational needs.

opt-in

Customers explicitly agree to having their habits tracked and/or to receive e-mail, and having to take action in order to grant this permission (via a radio button or sign-up form). Increasingly popular is the term "double opt-in," which involves an active confirmation of the original permission typically via e-mail.

opt-out

Customers agree to have habits tracked and/or to receive e-mail by accepting a company's terms and conditions of service, but have the ability to be removed from mailing lists or tracking by taking action to be removed (via radio button or e-mail/website request to unsubscribe).

organizational readiness

The willingness and ability of an organization to change its business focus, organizational structure and culture, metrics, processes, and procedures.

outsourcing
Managing a process or handling a function with external (vendor) resources and capabilities.

permission marketing
Most frequently used in an online context, an organization requests that a customer "opt-in" or provide permission to be contacted periodically with information or offers of specific interest or relevance.

point of sale/point of service (POS)
Refers to both the physical location where a transaction or customer interaction takes place, and the system used to process that transaction or interaction. This term has virtually replaced the term "cash register" in retail locations.

return on investment (ROI)
A measure of revenues generated (return) relative to expenses (investment).

sales force automation (SFA)
A broad term that refers to systems designed to support the ongoing activities of sales personnel. SFA tools typically support address book, scheduling, contact management, scripting, data collection and distribution, and reporting functions.

sales promotion
Any marketing initiative that has a primary objective of communicating a discount in price or a special offer designed to generate sales or interest in a product or service within a limited window of time.

scalability
A measure of how easily a given process, procedure, or system can grow.

segment manager

The role of an individual whose primary responsibilities include the acquisition, development, retention, and reactivation of a specific segment of customers.

segmentation

An intuitive or analytical process of dividing customers into mutually exclusive groups so that the customers within a group are maximally similar, while the groups are maximally dissimilar. Segmentation allows organizations to better understand customer lifecycles, and, therefore, the most appropriate development strategies to maximize customer value. Contact strategies are also typically tailored to the unique characteristics of each segment.

share of wallet

A measure of how much business a customer is giving you versus how much business they are spending in your category of product/service (or the sum total of business that they give to you and all of your competitors). This is often measured by product category or business line. Share of wallet could be considered a measure of customer loyalty, as well as customer potential.

up-sell

Proactively increasing the size of a customer's purchase by encouraging the purchase of a more expensive item or the purchase of an accessory. In service industries, up-sell usually translates to an increase in the rate of usage (e.g., cell phone usage) or balance (e.g., savings account balance) over a defined period of time.

INDEX

accuracy, data, 112, 113
Acquire and Retain (stage of CRM), 9–10
action, balancing planning with, 130
action plan, 47–48, 193
active customers, 194
ad targeting, 188
advertising, 54–55
analytical systems, 105
attrition, 194
automated voice response (AVR), 65
automation, marketing, 184–185
Automobile Club of Southern California, 14–15
AVR (automated voice response), 65

banking industry, 88–89, 92–94, 141–150
B2B, *see* business-to-business
B2C, *see* business-to-customer
Bell, Paul, on measuring customer experience, 30
Bluewater Technology Group Incorporated (case study), 163–172
    CRM implementation in, 167–170
    lessons learned in, 171–172
    situation overview for, 163–166
bottom-line benefits of CRM, 10–11
bottom-line business metrics, 125–127

boundaries, departmental/divisional, 107
business cases, 194
business focus
    gaps in, 45
    transformation of, 32–33
    see also focus
business intelligence, 194
business metrics, 73–86, 194
    customer-focused, 78–86, 199
    for customer loyalty and value, 77
    for customer revenues, 76
    for customer satisfaction, 76–77
    and data collection, 78
    and expansion of customer IQ, 78, 80–86
    gaps in, 45
    for place performance, 75
    for product performance, 74
    for program performance, 75
    transformation of, 34–35, 73–74
business model, 194
business rules, 195
business strategy, 57
business-to-business (B2B), 8, 53, 100, 195
business-to-customer (B2C), 195
Busquet, Ann, on "age of the customer," 17

207